BARKERBOOKS

POWERFUL AWAKENING
All rights reserved. © 2024, by F. CARO PONCE

Translated: Montserrat | BARKER BOOKS®
Book Cover and Interior Layout Design: Jorge Fernández | BARKER BOOKS®
Ilustration of cover: Bing

First Edition. Published by BARKER BOOKS®

I.S.B.N. Paperback | 979-8-89204-952-8
I.S.B.N. Hardcover | 979-8-89204-953-5
I.S.B.N. eBook | 979-8-89204-951-1

Library of Congress Copyrights Control Number 1-13455339212

No part of this publication may be reproduced, distributed, or transmitted in any form or by any means, including photocopying, recording, or other electronic or mechanical methods, without the prior written permission of the publisher, except in the case of brief quotations embodied in critical reviews and certain other noncommercial uses permitted by copyright law. For permission requests, write to the publisher, addressed "Attention: Permissions Coordinator," at the e-mail address below. The information, opinion, analysis and content of this book is the author's responsibility and it does not represent the point of view of the editorial company, BARKER BOOKS®.

BARKER BOOKS® and their affiliates are an imprint and registered trademark of Barker Publishing, LLC.

Printed in the United States

Barker Publishing, LLC
Los Angeles, California
https://barkerbooks.com
publishing@barkerbooks.com

POWERFUL AWAKENING
RENEW YOUR MIND AND TRANSFORM YOUR LIFE

F. CARO PONCE
PSYCHOLOGIST

CONTENTS

Introduction 7
Chapter 1 Getting to Know Yourself 11
Chapter 2 Releasing Baggage. Attachments and Forgiveness 33
Chapter 3 Inner Health 51
Chapter 4 The Brain's Extraordinary Design 71
Chapter 5 The Power of Thoughts 85
Chapter 6 The Creative Energy That Fills the Space 97
Chapter 7 Building a New Life 107
Chapter 8 The Powerful Law of Compensation 122
Chapter 9 Firm Mental Images 137
Chapter 10 Thinking > Feeling > Taking action
> Manifestation 147
Chapter 11 Smashing the Bronze Skies 163
Chapter 12 Accelerating Blessings 177

INTRODUCTION

Millions of people around the world have an empty, monotonous, numb experience of life. Most of the time, they feel that something is missing, that something is wrong; they are constantly restless. They get used to living without peace, without lasting joy. They become engrossed in the cyclical daily routine of surviving, working, paying bills, fulfilling obligations, and having brief and scarce moments of satisfaction. It seems that a part of their being is determined not to allow them to enjoy life. They live in an internal emotional war that they have not yet been able to overcome.

However, there is a powerful force within each of us that is unknown to the vast majority of people. This inner force has brought you to where you are now in your life. You can learn what it is and how it works and begin to use it to your advantage to transform yourself and build the life you have always desired. It's time to wake up to the joy of living.

The first step is to know your structure, how your mind works, and the power of your thoughts, to learn to free yourself from all limiting and rigid beliefs, from all emotional baggage from the past, and from all attachments that imprison and suffocate your true essence. By knowing yourself and understanding how the power implanted in your mind works to renew you, you can overcome whatever situation you are facing, have mastery over your emotions, and not allow them to rule you and direct your decisions. You can control your thoughts by focusing on creating, building yourself up, and not harming yourself. It is possible to be everything you have always wanted to be, to achieve the goals you set for yourself, and to do the things you love. You can improve in your relationships, work, finances, and emotions; in short, in every area.

It is also essential to know the infallible laws that govern the universe and our lives at all times and to learn to use them in your favor and not against you. It is perfectly possible to be happy and free from all pain, of all trauma, of all obstacles. You can learn to conquer yourself and be, do, and have all the good things you can dream of for yourself and your loved ones. With the precision and infallibility of the universal laws, you can change your inner and outer world. These laws do not fail; we fail by going against them or by not applying the principles by which they govern our lives.

For you who feel a burning desire to renew yourself, to transform yourself, to begin to live in fullness, in this book, you will learn how to do it, to stop pruning the branches and pull up from the roots everything that has hindered you; you will begin to sow in good soil and produce fruit a hundredfold. Here, you will learn, in a practical and straightforward way, both your own structure and the function of the laws of the universe and the power to renew your life experience.

This book, written in simple language to make it easy to read for anyone who has the firm purpose of renewing their existence, summarizes years of work, study, practice, and research that have transformed and continue to renew my own life, as well as those of thousands of people around the globe.

Life should be a fascinating and wonderful experience; it should be lived in abundance, and you must know that you are designed to make it so. To do this, you must first have a powerful awakening. Let's begin!

CHAPTER 1

GETTING TO KNOW YOURSELF

BODY, SOUL, AND SPIRIT

A long time ago, in a faraway place, there was a family that owned a small farm. All their lives, the father, mother, and their two children had worked from dawn to dusk to keep their farm afloat. But it seemed that all their hard work was not enough. Each day, their debts accumulated, shortages became more frequent, and they lived in constant anxiety, feeling worried and exhausted. However, they were determined to go out every day, looking for a solution, advice, or help to pay their debts and prevent losing their farm—the only property and source of income they had.

Thus, they undertook long and arduous journeys

throughout the kingdom, searching for a merchant wanting to buy more of the scarce products produced on their farm. Or perhaps they could find someone who would trust them to invest or lend them enough money to make necessary repairs, buy tools and equipment to better till the land, and adequately feed the animals. But each time, they came back to the same starting point. For years, they tried one thing and another, but to no avail.

One night, as they sat in front of the fireplace, emotionally and physically drained after a long, hard day, they talked about how difficult it was to maintain the farm. Suddenly, the father had a flash of light in his mind and began to reflect on how they were wasting their lives, focusing on what they did not want, on what was not right, and, therefore, ceasing to enjoy life as a family without fully living. He thought about how they were living numb, on automatic, day after day, year after year, and life was slipping away from them like a handful of water between their hands. He shared his thoughts with his wife and two children, who agreed with him.

That night, they decided to stop living in constant struggle and worry. Of course, they would continue with their occupations, but they would do so by enjoying every little thing, and whatever had to happen, so be it. Farm or no farm, they had each other; their hearts continued to beat, and that alone was reason enough to be well.

The next morning, everyone woke up with a new energy, smiling, knowing that something had changed and feeling an expectation that something good was about to happen to them. In the days that followed, they worked not only on the farm but also on letting go of every emotion of anxiety and worry. Every time a stressful thought tried to enter their minds, they eliminated it, focusing on something good, thanking the Creator for the fresh, clean air, for the food, for having a family, or for being alive.

Gradually, life became less heavy and monotonous and became more enjoyable; they understood that they were looking for inner stability in the wrong places. They allowed themselves short breaks during the day and began to laugh more, things that rarely happened before.

One day, after dinner, they sat down again in front of the fireplace with a nice cup of tea, but no longer to talk about debts, problems, or shortages, but simply to talk about nice things, to laugh, to enjoy and to be thankful for what they had at that moment. The father took a deep breath, feeling a great delight for the moment they were living and for seeing his family at peace. At last, they were building happy moments. Absorbed in these peaceful thoughts, he watched the fire in the fireplace when his gaze fell on a small chest on the mantelpiece. He remembered that it had been a gift from his grandmother and contained a beautiful, glittering red pebble. He got up from the armchair, picked up the chest, opened it, and thought that perhaps the pebble had some value; if so, the silver he could get for it would be worth more than having it as an ornament on the mantelpiece.

The next day, he got up very early in the morning, and without wasting any time, he undertook a trip to the capital of the kingdom, where he called on jewelers and merchants to evaluate the red stone. He received the most diverse opinions about it. Some said it was too small and rare to be of any value; others said it was too large to be a costly stone. Some even refused to examine it, thinking it was a waste of time. Those who thought better of it suggested that it might be worth a couple of silver coins.

Finally, he went to the royal jeweler. He handed him the stone, now somewhat skeptical after the discouraging opinions he had received. After a long and meticulous investigation, it turned out that the stone was a rare, peculiar, and extremely valuable red diamond. The royal jeweler remarked to the man that surely the king would be interested in having such a stone, for there was nothing like it in all the royal treasuries. So they both went to the doors of the king's palace and requested an audience, which was granted because it was the royal jeweler. When the king saw the diamond, he was delighted with such a magnificent and extraordinary jewel, expressing his desire to buy it immediately, and he then gave the man five hundred gold coins for the red diamond. He hurried back to his farm, excited to tell his family what had happened.

Of course, the amount of gold he received was more than enough to pay off all their debts and save the farm, which was remodeled and restored to its former splendor. The family, which had been asleep at the wheel of daily worries and in great emotional oppression, finally lived happily and prosperously, not only financially but also inwardly, free from internal burdens and sharing with others the many blessings that followed them all the days of their lives.

I wrote this story to illustrate what happens to us very often and to reflect that, like the family in the story, we look for the solution in the wrong places and with the wrong attitude when, in fact, the solution lies within each of us.

This family sat every night in front of the red diamond, complaining about the bad things and focusing on them. But the answer they were looking for was right in front of them and inside them all the time; they just needed a change of attitude.

Not knowing the value of something can make us ignore it, minimize it, or even despise it. However, in the case of this family, everything began to change when they decided to concentrate on seeing the good and what they had instead of focusing on the lack.

The solution to any conflict or situation you may be going through begins within you. There is a red diamond within you, a power given to you to overcome any obstacle so you can renew your entire life. We are not mere spectators in our own lives; rather, we hold the responsibility and possess the power to change ourselves and, in doing so, design and attract the life we want.

To discover that power—that red diamond—and to use it correctly, you must know yourself and how your mind, soul, and consciousness work.

The purpose of this book is not to explain the information presented here in a scientific, detailed, and profound way but to present, in the simplest way and with easy-to-understand language, the infallible laws that govern us, as well as the general functioning of the human being, to understand our structure and to apply simple steps to transform our lives in the best way.

Let us now consider the three entities that make up our being: body, soul, and spirit.

BODY

The body is where the basic needs are: sleeping, eating, drinking water, grooming, dressing, evacuating, resting, and so on. The body must be attended to and cared for correctly since it is the only one we will have during our life in this world. On many occasions, abusing or neglecting it reflects self-rejection and low self-esteem.

As we will see later, bad sleeping and eating habits, not doing some kind of exercise, neglecting hygiene, or not getting adequate rest are factors that affect our emotions and thinking. We must learn to know ourselves, accept and love ourselves, and correct the bad habits we have at this moment in order to reach a level of integral well-being. The body is the house where the soul and the spirit live.

SOUL

The soul is where the personality, will, mind, emotions, tastes, and preferences reside. The soul can receive direction or influence through the spirit, which is the internal part that awakens consciousness, or from the outer part that comes through the five senses and which the brain analyzes and classifies according to past experiences.

The mind is greatly influenced by the ego, which is mistakenly thought to be the "self" of the person, but this is not so. The ego has nothing to do with self-esteem or self-confidence; on the contrary, it damages self-esteem and makes the person insecure.

The ego is that voice in your mind that sounds like you and makes you believe it is your own voice, but it is not you. It is an intruder that tries to dominate the mind and constantly inclines it towards the negative, the fatalistic, the bad, and the external. Your true essence is to be in a state of consciousness.

Because the ego manifests itself as that voice in the mind that sounds similar to our voice, it makes us believe that we are the ones who think, believe, and want what it suggests to us in the mind. When we listen and obey its suggestions through the thoughts it implants, we cease to be aware of our true nature. It is as if our lives are being governed by someone else while we remain numb and observant. That is why it is extremely important to know all this, to learn to distinguish the voice of the ego from the voice of your consciousness, which is your true "self."

Although the ego is not your true essence, your free will—which is the freedom to choose—always continues to operate, and so decisions are made by your free will, being your responsibility and your choice. The ego proposes, but it cannot force us to make decisions. You can begin today to control your choices from your consciousness. As you progress through the reading, you will have more clarity about the steps you need to take to awaken your consciousness and renew your life.

The ego is not conscious and is generally focused on the external. It is based mainly on emotions such as fear, guilt, anger, and sadness, from which many more arise. Obviously, we are emotional beings, and we can feel fear in a positive way. For example, in the face of real danger, fear helps us to survive. However, the ego focuses mostly on imaginary things that 95% of the time do not happen.

We can also feel guilt for mistakes we have made, and, in a healthy sense, this helps us to correct, learn from the mistake, be responsible, and modify our actions. On the contrary, the ego uses guilt as a daily habit to wear the person down, and as it is not conscious, no changes are generated, and it is not corrected; there is only remorse that brings insecurity, discouragement, and, in the long run, depression. Also, the sadness produced from the spirit helps us correct our path and make wise decisions. But the sadness of the ego leads to depression.

We can also experience anger, which helps us to motivate ourselves for positive change and to make the right decisions. In the ego, on the other hand, anger overflows and is generalized toward everyone and everything, including themselves.

The ego's focus is on the negative. It focuses on the past to constantly bring to mind painful, difficult memories that cause guilt, dissatisfaction, unforgiveness, rejection, insecurity, anger, and sadness. When it is not in the past, it moves into the future, bringing thoughts of fear, anguish, and anxiety, fatalistic thoughts that something terrible might happen to themselves or someone close to them.

We are not designed to dwell on the past or worry about the future, so this constant ego activity in the mind causes exhaustion and imbalance. In order to be in the present we have to be conscious; we cannot be conscious in the past or in the future.

The ego focuses on the present only to escape from

itself and does so in search of momentary pleasure. It does not care what price it pays later as long as it gets immediate pleasure. For example, binge eating junk food, pornography, illicit relationships, gossiping, spending money one does not have to go shopping, or getting into debt. It always acts in an emotional and uncontrolled way. It takes over the mind, imprisons the soul, and numbs the conscience.

Every time you give in to your ego's desires, you are only making it stronger, and everything you give to the ego produces addiction and emptiness; that is to say, the satisfaction you receive lasts only a moment, and you feel an emptiness again and the need to fill it with the external, which pushes you to a never-ending cycle of the same and more of it. This is the origin of addictions of all kinds: drugs, alcohol, food, social networks, work, and material things, among many others.

When people are in the ego, they cannot work on themselves to heal internally because they live in the unconscious.

The ego gravitates towards two opposite extremes; it does not know how to have a balance in practically anything. One extreme is when a person becomes completely self-centered and frivolous and does not think of others to contribute or help. When asked to do something that doesn't directly benefit them, they may forget about it or perform it halfheartedly, simply out of obligation, hoping to gain some sort of reward or approval.

They develop an explosive and violent temperament, in which they are instantly dominated by their emotions when faced with any external event. They respond with anger, sarcasm, or mockery and do things to be noticed.

The ego is fed when emotions are not healed, when internal conflicts have been dragging on for years, and makes the person feel inferior, and tries to compensate for it by having a higher self-concept of reality. They lie and exaggerate things to aggrandize themselves and present themselves as someone who knows everything. They ask questions not to learn but to answer themselves, seeking self-exaltation and showing everything they claim to know. They think they deserve everything good without being responsible for anything.

They use blackmail, flattery, and manipulation of emotions to control others, even using gifts and material things to force others to do what the ego wants. However, all these approaches only generate more emptiness and internal disorder. The person is unhappy, suffers, feels imprisoned, and is unsatisfied.

At the other extreme, the person is overly empathic because their self-esteem is significantly damaged, and, without realizing it, they desperately seek to compensate for this low self-esteem with approval through what others think of them. They do not know how to be assertive; they say yes when they really mean no and vice versa. They are easily influenced, neglect their emotional and mental health and well-being to help others, and say yes to everything. If at any time they say no to someone else's request, they feel guilty for the rest of the day and are tormented in their mind by the ego.

At both extremes, the ego inclines the person to seek external approval; they want to be admired in one way or another. It is all busyness and appearance in the ego. The person lives trying to please others and striving to make them think of them as something they are not. Sometimes, the person even loses their dignity to receive approval. They dress, speak, and do things that make them feel uncomfortable just to fit in and please others; they lose their identity.

This toxic cycle is a continuous drain of energy, leaving the person feeling emotionally exhausted and tired. One tends to go through life without being fully present, resulting in a monotonous and routine existence, and tasks are done automatically and heavily.

Balance is the right thing to do. We do our part to help those who need it without neglecting our inner work, our emotional health. Because if you're not well, you can't help others to be well either.

The ego does not know how to listen or be at rest. It is always anxious, troubled, or worried about something, bringing to mind constant emotional noise. Its nature is busyness and restlessness.

There is no true love in the ego; there are only habits, obligations, demands, expectations, and attachments (which we will discuss in the next chapter). The ego cannot love freely since it is driven by fear, and as a result, a person cannot truly love oneself.

The lack of self-love produces self-rejection, which in turn inclines the person to focus on the external to receive approval and compensate for internal voids through achievements, material things, appearance, relationships, pleasures, and attention-seeking. Their emotions govern their lives, making them rise and fall abruptly.

The ego focuses on what it lacks, on what it does not have, on the negative, on the bad things that other people do, and on correcting others in an attempt to evade correcting itself. The person is miserable, likes drama, seeks to feel offended, takes everything personally, is vindictive, and does not know how to let go or forgive. They are always thinking about what they do not want; therefore, they give it strength and attract it more and more.

Although it may seem overwhelming, it is necessary to know how the ego operates in the soul through the mind to unmask it and remove all control.

As long as the ego dominates the mind, there will always be an endless flow of negative and unhealthy thoughts that plunge the person into exhaustion, constant stress, and endless mental noise. They victimize themselves all the time, self-justify, and blame people, circumstances, things, and everything, avoiding accepting the responsibility to change. Of course, we have all gone through difficult and painful circumstances, but as we will learn in the following chapters, we have the power to overcome any adversity and direct our lives toward inner healing.

This inner enemy loves to procrastinate, that is, to leave things for later, especially those that have to do with self-reflection, inner work, and everything that leads to an awakening of the spirit, of consciousness. It makes quite a show to keep the mind busy with worries and chores.

Although the person may appear very organized, when the ego is in control, there will always be areas of disorganization, whether in eating habits, sleep, exercise, finances, closet, car, or relationships.

Almost always, the external is a reflection of the internal. Clutter adds more mental and emotional chaos, which the ego loves because it is material to continue to overwhelm the mind. The more the soul soothes down, the more we seek order and simplicity in life, and the more we learn to enjoy the little things and to be in the present.

People in the ego will have a square perspective. They will judge anyone who does not think as they do or who does not share their ideas or beliefs, and they will not know how to respect; instead, they will criticize and attack. They are stubborn and obstinate. This causes them to have a limited and rigid appreciation of life in general. They walk with a magnifying glass in their hand, looking for and magnifying the mistakes of others, finding faults, and focusing on the negative.

Consciousness, which is the true essence, is turned off. Therefore, the person is not living their own life; they are numb and hypnotized, believing that their ego is their true self and following all its harmful desires. In this state, the soul is imprisoned, burdened, and tired, as if living a bad dream and struggling to wake up.

Remember that all this is the ego wanting to rule over your mind and emotions. Until now, you had assumed that voice was yours and followed its suggestions, but it is time to wake up. It is time to learn how to turn off this harmful voice, this repetitive and toxic computer program that has limited you and made you suffer all your life.

SPIRIT

The human spirit plays a crucial role in awakening consciousness, which is the true "self" of the person. It serves as a bridge between us and the infinite source of love, peace, and joy. It helps you to stay in the present, as it is the greatest source of nourishment for the consciousness. Essentially, it is the voice of your being that orients you towards the positive and helps you to reflect in a focused way. Here, you develop self-control so that instead of being ruled by your emotions, you are able to regulate yourself, control your emotions, and direct them in a healthy and conscious way toward what is right.

Self-esteem is based on the spirit, on the internal, on the soul, and on the essence of the person. On the contrary, the ego tries to base self-esteem on external factors like appearances, approval, accomplishments, and things that feed it for a moment but leave a deep sense of emptiness and dissatisfaction in the soul. Self-esteem is not something that is built or nourished from the outside but from within, in the spirit, in the consciousness.

The spirit helps the soul stay in the present, in a state of consciousness where the person stops listening to the suggestive voice of the ego and begins to take responsibility for their own mind. When the ego shuts down, consciousness awakens; only then can we sort out the direction of our lives and begin to really live.

In the ego, there is no fixed, safe, or positive direction; life revolves around the past, the future, the bad of the present, negative emotions overflowing, and a focus on the external, circumstances, people, or material things. When you don't know where to go, any path can seem right, even if its end is destructive.

DETHRONING THE EGO

The first step in dethroning the ego is to discover it, to know that this voice is not you so that you can enter into a voluntary state of consciousness in which you begin to question the ideas it suggests and the orders it tries to impose on your mind to incline you towards the negative. Thus, we go from a life of lethargy, from doing things automatically and unconsciously, and from being impulsive people, victims of our own ego-mind, to being conscious people, with full will, responsible and with self-control, choosing the thoughts that are allowed in the mind and those that are not.

With every thought, every emotion, every word, every action, at every moment, we are either feeding the ego or feeding the spirit, strengthening one and weakening the other. The ego cannot seek the things of the spirit because it completely blocks the mind to it. In the past, you may not have had this knowledge, so you automatically obeyed every suggestion of your mind, believing that you were directing yourself; in this way, the ego was constantly being fed without you realizing it while your spirit was in partial or total fasting. Now, however, you can consciously focus on this task, which is the first step towards your transformation.

There are infinite ways in which your spirit can be fed, and the better fed it is and the more attention you pay to it, the more your consciousness rises, the more you awaken, and the more the ego shuts down; that is the key to everything. Of course, it goes without saying that the primary way to nourish your spirit is to connect with the Eternal Creator, the one who designed you and implanted in you that help, that guide, that power for you to awaken your consciousness and take charge of your life, not the ego, which is a harmful intruder.

You also feed your spirit every time you laugh at good things, when you enjoy your family and the people you love, when you are aware of the present moment, when you play with your pets, when you enjoy nature, when you go for a walk, when you read things that bring you something positive and help you in your process of renewing your mind. When you spend moments alone and enjoy your own company without the need for noise, when you reflect and meditate on the good, every thought focused and conscious on the positive, on the pure, on what you do want, every feeling of hope, of love, of peace, of inner happiness. When you expect something good to happen, you feed your spirit, strengthening your consciousness and weakening the ego.

Take at least thirty minutes every day for yourself to relax, meditate, or enjoy a cup of tea or coffee. Listen to the voice of your spirit, and you will gradually learn to distinguish it from the voice of the ego. Love yourself and treat yourself with kindness. What you would like others to do for you, start doing it for yourself.

It is important to note that as long as we live in this world, the ego will try to take control of the mind. It won't shut down and never come back, but it will be waiting for any opportunity where it can cleverly disguise its attacks with suggestions of the thousand things you should be worrying about or creating excessive busyness to exhaust you, to make you lazy to feed your spirit and put your focus on the outer. Thus, it immediately returns to taking your mind hostage and directing your life toward the negative.

Any moment of difficulty you may go through, or when something doesn't go right, the ego will quickly take advantage of it and will try to control your thoughts again. Don't let it; be aware of the thoughts you let into your mind. Remember that when the ego rules you, you stop living because you enter into a state of unconsciousness of the present moment and begin to live in automatic, always busyness.

One tactic it uses is to sow fear of the new, of change, of being free, prosperous, and truly happy; it blames you and wants you to live in misery, in anger, and in dramas built out of nothing. It is your greatest tormentor and the one who has generated in your life the most significant damage and emotional pain. Its greatest power is to impersonate you and make you believe it is you. It is time to strip it of all power and be aware; it is time to begin to recognize your own inner voice, the voice of your spirit.

What is truly reassuring is that the more you put your will into nurturing your spirit and staying in consciousness, the easier it will be to identify the ego's attacks and the less intense and less frequent they will become because your own spirit, yourself in your awareness will be in command of the mind to self-direct it toward the healthy and positive.

Your life takes the shape of what is in your mind. For your life to change, it is not necessary to strive to change the external circumstances or the people around you; that would be too tiring and exhausting. All your focus should be on yourself, on doing inner work. As you are being renewed and transformed, it will seem that everything around you is also being renewed and transformed, and actually, it is.

Only by positioning ourselves in the spirit can consciousness truly awaken and remain in that state. When we reach this state of consciousness where the mind is free of ego—because we learn to discern and choose the thoughts we want—we can live happily, in freedom, enjoying what we do in our daily lives. Life ceases to be cyclical, heavy, and stressful and becomes enjoyable; even the colors seem brighter.

No dream can ever compare to the reality of being awake. You can be happy, live in inner peace, and advance and prosper in everything. When you have lived governed by the ego, this may seem unbelievable, yet it is perfectly and simply possible. In reality, a state of well-being, love, peace, and happiness is the normal human state; the ego has hindered this state and created chaos and suffering in the mind.

The ego has sold you the idea that there is a part of you that can't, that is weak, that doesn't know, that deserves to suffer and live with lack, or that you are prone to feeling insecure, depressed, or anxious, that something bad will always overshadow whatever good happens to you, or that you need the approval of others to feel good. All that is the voice of the ego; it is a description of itself, but the ego is not you. Listening to it and believing it is the basis of all internal suffering.

The worst tragedy in the life of any human being is to spend a lifetime believing that you are the ego, controlled and manipulated by your own mind, preventing you from living in fullness, thinking that all the mental noise and its endless negative narratives are your own voice and that this is the normal of life. No! We all need to have a powerful awakening of consciousness in the depths of our spirit so that the voice of the ego dissipates and, along with it, all the unnecessary suffering that had enslaved us for so many years.

It is essential to make it a priority to nourish the spirit in order to awaken the consciousness and to remain in this state of analysis of thoughts to choose the right ones. Just as the immune system detects, recognizes, and attacks any external invader that threatens the well-being of your body, from now on, you must remain in consciousness to identify harmful thoughts and intruders of the ego.

Changes achieved without nurturing the spirit are like pruning the branches of a tree, which will eventually grow back and become stronger. True, deep, and permanent changes occur by uprooting everything from the root.

Beginning to live in the present, in the consciousness from the spirit, triggers a self-construction mechanism that automatically releases emotions repressed for years, and the roots of old harmful habits begin to weaken.

One of the basic functions of the mind is to choose. We will always have at least two options to choose from: to believe the ego's negative suggestions or to listen to our authentic inner voice in the spirit and be aware. Whatever is good, whatever is pure, whatever is kind, whatever is good for us, whatever helps us to change, to renew ourselves, to awaken, to love, to enjoy daily life, to transform ourselves, this is what we should think about.

CHAPTER 2

RELEASING BAGGAGE. ATTACHMENTS AND FORGIVENESS

On one occasion, I was at the airport in the city of Denver, Colorado. It was winter, and the morning temperature was particularly cold; a few inches of snow had fallen during the night, and at that moment, sleet was falling. Several planes were lined up on the runway, waiting for their turn to take off. The technical staff sprayed each plane with a mixture of water and glycol to melt the snow and slow down the formation of ice. From the plane window, I could see everything frozen all around; the sky was covered with thick gray clouds, everything seemed paralyzed, and although it was early in the morning, it seemed late.

When it was our turn to take off, we began to lift off and suddenly found ourselves with zero visibility due to dark clouds laden with snow and ice. When the plane had gained enough altitude, we changed to a completely different panorama. Above the clouds, the sun was shining brightly, illuminating the horizon with vibrant colors. The blue color of the sky was deep and clean, and down below, the clouds even looked bright and white. All was calm. Above, the storm was no more.

In the same way as this experience, we can assimilate what happens when a life becomes burdened with emotional baggage. When attachments and unforgiveness take root, they can freeze everything around, rendering life gray and devoid of joy. The constant happiness that once shone brightly is now hidden, and the individual's focus is on finding external sources of relief to break through the freeze, even if only temporarily.

To really live and enjoy daily life, we must forgive, free ourselves from unnecessary burdens, and let go of all attachments. Only then can we rise above the storm and see that up there, the sun is shining, and the sky is bluer.

Carrying a heavy burden in the soul is one of the most exhausting things in life, and even worse when you do not know how to get rid of it. This heavy emotional baggage eventually becomes physical ailments in the body, from stomach problems, allergies, and asthma to heart complications, anxiety crises, and depression, among many others.

All emotions are already within us and are activated with a particular thought; when they are activated, they become feelings. If you think of something you like very much, it will trigger an emotion of well-being and happiness, making you feel very good. If you think about something difficult and painful that happened to you in the past or something that hurt you, it will trigger a negative emotion that will make you feel bad. There are no neutral thoughts; they are either positive or negative, and all, without exception, affect your organism, your whole being, and your environment. As we will examine in Chapter 5, thoughts are cumulative, and they have a weight that is added and strengthened the more we think about something in particular.

I use this exercise with my patients to better understand the effect of thoughts on our organism. If possible, I would like you to do it now.

Close your eyes for a moment and imagine that you are holding a lemon in your hand. Now, imagine taking a knife with your other hand and cutting it in half. Imagine that it is so juicy that when you cut it, the juice jumps out. Visualize the color and texture of the lemon inside, and bring your hand to your mouth, imagining that you squeeze it and drink its juice.

Surely, if you concentrated, you salivated when you imagined the lemon juice in your mouth. With a small exercise that took you less than a minute, you presented, so to speak, a psychosomatic manifestation: a thought produced a reaction in your organism. Imagine what a negative thought can do if it is carried in your mind all day, or for a week, or for a month, or for years. It will undoubtedly have tremendous negative consequences.

RELEASING BAGGAGE

We cannot prevent things from happening that affect us, but by understanding how to deal with them, we can let go instead of accumulating burdens. Emotions are not to be repressed, they are not to be ignored, they are not to be fought against, they are not to be kept, they must be released in a healthy way. Whatever is kept in the subconscious without being healed, without being worked on, the body will later externalize it in the form of diseases. The things that the heart is silent about, the body will shout them out later.

To release an unnecessary burden, you must first detect it, which can only be achieved by being in awareness and turning off the ego's voice. One way to help release negative emotions is to imagine the incident that troubled you in the way you would have liked it to happen. Thus, the subconscious stores that experience as real and releases the emotional charge instead of repressing it, and helps you to be better prepared in the future to act correctly.

You can also write a letter expressing everything you

need to say, both to yourself and to the person with whom you had the conflict, then imagine that you are in front of them and tell them what you wrote. Finally, you can tear or burn the letter, consciously letting go of everything that hurts you. It may be necessary to do these exercises several times at first, but no effort is too much when it comes to our emotional health, which is the foundation of a fulfilling life. Throughout the book, you will find other exercises to help you in this area.

ATTACHMENTS

In the simplest way, an attachment is when you put your emotional stability into a person, a circumstance, something material, or something external and depend on it for your well-being. Your focus and energy are on it, your life revolves around it, and you make decisions around it.

The whole basis of attachments is fear. The person is afraid of losing the object of their addiction, their supposed happiness, and their emotional stability, thinking that without it, they cannot be well. In reality, it is the attachment that prevents one from being truly happy. Let us look at some of the different types of attachments.

It is important to note that any or all of the characteristics described below may be present, but not necessarily all of them must be present for it to be considered an attachment.

EMOTIONAL ATTACHMENT

Dependence develops in relationships, whether romantic, familial, or social. The person depends on someone else to feel good and to make decisions, however small they may be. They seek approval in everything; they lose their individuality and the ability to be assertive. They do not know how to say no, even when it affects them, and they become insecure and dependent. The person creates enormous expectations and demands around the person with whom the attachment has developed.

They become invasive, do not know how to respect the space of others, and are always after the other person. They look for excuses to be in constant contact with the other person in order to receive a dose of approval and attention. Even if the relationship is not working well, the attachment is so strong that they prefer any kind of attention, even if it is negative, to receiving nothing at all.

If they are in a group, they want to be the focus of the other's attention. They analyze and carefully study every move the person they have become attached to makes because they don't want anyone else to be above them in the other person's life. They become obsessive and make constant demands because they want more attention. Without realizing it, they become addicted to the other person.

The person may feel victimized, devalued, and dependent, believing they need the other person to be well.

Over time, they may resort to manipulation, blackmail, lies, tantrums, and drama to maintain the other person's presence. Even if the result is an argument, the ego makes them feel that they received their daily dose of attachment, and now they have material to meditate in their mind all day long, recreating the scene over and over again, imagining and arguing in their mind with someone who is not present at that moment. The more they think about it, the more they victimize themselves and the more attachment they feel, strengthening the cycle of addiction, emptiness, and fear.

Sometimes, there is a mixture of anger and affection, a desire to pull away and let go of the other person, and an apparent need to keep the other person close. They go from blaming themselves for behaving the way they do not want to behave to victimizing themselves, convincing themselves that they are right. This creates confusion in their minds, and they feel an overwhelming emotional burden that they struggle to handle.

A negative, toxic thought pattern develops, distorting reality and making people see things very differently. This is one of the most common attachments, and it should be noted that the ego intervenes so that the person does not accept that they have it.

MATERIAL ATTACHMENT

The origin of this attachment lies in the inner or emotional voids, in low self-esteem, which unconsciously seeks to be filled with material things. It may be due to a lack of affection, recognition, poor self-perception, or self-rejection in the body or in some other area.

The person seeks to present themselves as confident and competes with others without their knowledge. They may come across as self-assured, but deep down, they feel lonely, empty, and insecure. They evaluate their own worth based on their possessions and judge others in the same manner. This leads them to be overly critical of themselves and those around them, constantly making comparisons.

In this attachment, the ego is constantly detonating feelings of frustration, dissatisfaction, anger, anxiety, loneliness, and emotional and physical exhaustion. The person lives asleep, out of consciousness, and fails to understand that everything material and the satisfaction it produces is temporary. Trying to fill internal voids with external things only increases the emptiness. It is impossible to permanently extinguish an attachment without nourishing the spirit and allowing the consciousness to awaken.

People with this attachment are generally deceived by their ego, feeling rejection and putting up barriers to their own spirit; they relate it to religiosity, which is the farthest thing from the truth. Religiosity is caused by the ego's effort to convince the person that fulfilling certain requirements or steps will be the right thing to do in their spirit, but they never find freedom or redemption for their soul.

As we saw in the previous chapter, nourishing the spirit involves awakening consciousness, relating directly to the Creator of all things, enjoying life in a healthy way, and loving oneself first to then be able to give love to others.

We all need material things to live well: a good house, a car, good clothes, good food, money to vacation and take care of our bodies, to be able to share with others and help those in need. It is okay to want to progress and improve in life; what is not right is to depend on external things for your well-being, to judge your value as a person by material things, to cling to things by making them a priority, or to base your success in life on the amount of money or material things you accumulate.

In many cases, people do things unconsciously, thinking of others to pretend, be admired, and show off. All this is the work of the ego in the mind. The more material things they accumulate, the more their attachment grows, and now they are afraid of losing what was supposed to bring them well-being. In the end, they enter into a state of anxiety and uneasiness.

AVOIDANT ATTACHMENT

In this type of attachment, the person strives at all costs not to lose their independence. They avoid forming serious and deep relationships. They repress emotions and feelings and hide their needs so as not to feel vulnerable, incapable, or inferior. Deep down, they are afraid of being hurt, so they pretend that everything is fine, that things don't matter so much to them, and that they can do everything on their own without needing anyone else.

They always seek to be in control of everything around them, which causes them a lot of insecurity, anxiety, stress, sadness, exhaustion, and loneliness. In our society, no one can be completely independent; we all need each other in different ways, from receiving a service or a product to the need to feel loved, appreciated, respected, and valued.

When awakening to consciousness, we can express our feelings in a healthy way without hurting or blaming others. As the ego is extinguished, the person no longer takes everything personal and no longer feels that everyone wants to take advantage of them or hurt them. Their interpersonal relationships improve, especially their relationship with themselves, from which they can heal and not be afraid.

As we move forward in the process of becoming more conscious, we can clearly understand when other people are prey to the ego in their minds, and instead of blaming, judging, or pointing fingers, we feel great compassion and the need to help them in their process. We all, without exception, need a powerful awakening to be free and to heal.

SELF-CONCEPT ATTACHMENT

It is a limiting and ingrained belief about oneself imposed by the ego that the person has accepted as their reality, defining them in a restrictive, negative, and limited way. Essentially, it is a person's perception of themselves from the perspective of their ego.

They convince themselves that they cannot overcome bad habits, addictions, or attachments and that they cannot change or overcome themselves; they feel inferior and incapable. They use phrases such as "I have always been like this," "I have always believed this," "This is how I was taught," "I am like this, and I am not going to change," "I can't," "I don't know how," "At this point, you can't change." This attachment increases insecurity, low self-esteem, self-doubt, fear, feelings of inferiority, guilt, self-rejection, and more. They try to compensate with the appearance of security, that they are happy just as they are.

There are other types of attachments, but these examples are sufficient to understand how they operate unconsciously in the ego-ridden soul.

PRACTICING DETACHMENT

As with addictions, in order to get rid of attachments, become emotionally free, and heal yourself, the first step is to recognize that you have them. We must be extremely honest and open. Even if you think you have no attachments or any of the things we will see below, it is always important to do a self-analysis. Just being open to the possibility that there are things to change and baggage to release through conscious analysis is enlightening. If this is not the case and there is nothing to change and nothing to let go of, tomorrow you can go back to the same starting point you were at.

However, I must point out that in the process of renewing the mind, we all have to heal something, let go of some kind of attachment, and correct our thoughts and behavior. There is no human being who does not have to do some work to overcome their greatest enemy, which is the ego in their mind, and the best and fastest way to do it is to start by recognizing that we need help, to be humble and honest with ourselves.

Attachments are like strong sedatives that keep the consciousness asleep and unbalance the emotions. If someone tries to tell the person that they have some attachment to something, the ego immediately goes to war and will say it is not so; it will put phrases in the mind like, "But I don't do all that stuff," "I think they are exaggerating," "It is not an attachment, it is something normal," "It is not that big of a deal." Then they victimize themselves, feeling offended and minimizing things because the ego has, above all, a distorted vision of reality.

The person is in lethargy, denial, and self-deceived by the ego, which takes control of thoughts and emotions. All attachment begins in the ego and ends in the spirit as consciousness awakens.

Detachment is fostered by consciously letting go of the need to want to control things, people, or circumstances, by recognizing that you have been clinging to something to fill inner voids, and by understanding that you were being guided by fear rather than love and trust. Letting go does not mean that you stop caring or loving, but that you begin to love yourself, dignify, love, and respect the person you were attached to, giving space and freedom. You will be surprised how learning to let go makes everything better.

Accepting yourself is a big step in letting go of attachments. You cannot fight against yourself; you must love, accept, and forgive yourself for all your past mistakes. Start over from scratch today. This is an inner work.

I have attended hundreds of people who describe themselves as someone who knows how to listen, is empathic, loves, and likes to help others. But let's stop and think about how much you love yourself, how empathetic you are to yourself, and how much you listen to yourself. Perhaps you thought you were listening to yourself all your life, but in reality, it was the voice of your ego deceiving you.

Maybe what you have been looking for in other people is a lack of affection from yourself. Start pampering yourself, treat yourself well, and don't wait for others to do for you what you are not doing for yourself.

Take control of your mind and focus on something other than the object of your attachment. Take a course or a class, go out for a coffee, go to the park, read something that contributes and helps you grow, think of ways in which you can nourish your spirit and awaken your consciousness, and enjoy your company. Practice saying no when you feel it is right and saying yes when it is what you want.

The ego is possessive, so it does not want to let go of attachments. But as you work on your mind, you begin to find within yourself what you were looking for outside, and you let go of the emotional addiction, the possessiveness towards a person or thing. Seek personal goals and your own objectives; do not seek external approval.

FORGIVENESS

Forgiveness is a decision that is made from the consciousness, from the spirit. In the ego, it is impossible to truly forgive because, deep down, the person has not even forgiven themselves. The ego clings to the past, to relationships, customs, things, places, habits, and offenses, repeating them over and over again in the mind, magnifying and reviving emotions of anger, resentment, desire for revenge, victimization and clinging more and more to the offense.

Not forgiving is another of the heaviest emotional burdens a person can carry. It can lead to an infinity of ailments and illnesses; it is very serious and deteriorates the body, soul, and spirit.

To forgive is not to justify or condone what others did,

nor is it to minimize or ignore the damage; instead, it is to make a decision from your conscience, with your will, to break the bond that binds you to another person. Forgiveness allows you to let go of the burden that weighs you down and stops you from being free and experiencing peace. It is not for the other person's benefit but for your own well-being. And, of course, this process includes forgiving yourself.

Everything has to be done from the spirit, from the consciousness. If you try to forgive from the ego, you get into a battle where the ego will try to convince you that you are right not to want to forgive and that it is your right to hold on to it. The more you try to push out the emotion of unforgiveness, the more it takes root inside of you because what you are trying to push out of your life, you are actually pushing it inside you; when you put all your energy into pushing something away, you inadvertently give it more power over you.

Everything is a struggle in the ego, while in your spirit, everything flows and is easy. Therefore, the first step is to work on awakening your consciousness, feeding your spirit, and learning to distinguish your own voice from the voice of the ego. Remember that this is not you and that you have the power to choose freely.

If we stop right now to analyze what we are carrying on our backs, we will notice that it is excessive and unnecessary baggage. Of course, these are things we are not even aware of.

Understanding that the power is in the choices we consciously make will begin to dramatically change your life. Right now, you can choose to let go of the drudgery of wanting to control everything, of trying to solve everything for others, and of clinging to people or things to be okay. The body is under constant stress when the mind is busy trying to be in control of the whole environment; it enters a state of alertness where energy leaks out.

DEVELOP THE HABIT OF LETTING GO QUICKLY

When things don't go as planned or as you would have liked, it's important to let go quickly. There's nothing wrong with that. Correct what you can and move forward in the present; do not let the ego keep spinning in your mind the things that have already happened. What happened yesterday is already past; your life consists of small instants of the present, nothing more, that's all you have. When you get stuck in the past, you stop living, and you go into a kind of self-hypnosis where life escapes without you realizing it; it is the ego ruling the mind.

Excessive thoughts of the past or anxiety about things in the future constitute extra weight in the baggage you carry. No transformation can occur in the past because it is a non-existent time. Change and renewal happen in the present.

It is not your responsibility to solve everything, nor to live for others the process that is theirs to live; let go of the baggage that is not yours. Your first responsibility is to work on your inner self, not the circumstances or the people around you. As you move forward in your awakening of consciousness through your spirit, your environment also begins to improve, and in this way, you can help awaken others, which is the greatest benefit we can bring to those we love.

Unexpected events, situations beyond our control, can happen every day. Sometimes, these difficult circumstances, the stages of suffering and crisis, can be the most productive moments that move us to a powerful awakening because they force us to stop, reflect, rectify, and think about a change. Suffering purifies the soul, helps us connect with our spirit, and awaken our consciousness.

All external situations are 10%; your reaction to them represents 90%. You decide if you see it with the mind of the ego and make it big, allowing it to spoil the rest of your day and your present moments. Or if you see it with the mind of your true essence, from your spirit, and react rationally, focused on the solution, choosing healthy thoughts that activate healthy emotions. You work on it in the moment, then let go and move on with your life.

Most of our problems, mistakes, and bad decisions are caused by following the ego's voice, which we often mistake as our own; consequently, we do not resist and do not control our impulses. The greatest suffering in life is caused by our own mind, but these problems are

95% eliminated when we wake up and listen to our true voice in the spirit.

Every Experience is a Learning Experience, a Blessing in Disguise

During the attack on the Twin Towers in New York, there were many people whose lives were saved because of some incident that at that moment they saw as something negative. People who were delayed because they spilled their coffee, lost their keys, got stuck in traffic, or missed their train. At the time, they were irritated; they didn't see any good in it. The ego took over and unleashed dozens of dramatic thoughts, but then they were grateful, amazed at how a negative incident resulted in something good and even saved their lives.

Every difficult event presents us with an opportunity to learn, return to awareness, and maintain self-control over all negative emotions. By expressing gratitude for everything, even if we don't understand the reason behind it in the moment, we are freeing ourselves from the weight of burdens instead of piling them on our backs. Gratitude is an excellent tool for letting go of unnecessary emotional and mental baggage.

Everything happens for the best when your spirit is being nourished and your consciousness is awakening; even if all you can see are the thick gray clouds for the moment, you can rise above them, and the sun will shine again.

CHAPTER 3

INNER HEALTH

REPLACING LIMITING BELIEFS

Some time ago, during a beautiful autumn afternoon, I went for a stroll along the Champs-Élysées in Paris. As I walked along the busy and elegant cafés and luxury stores that fill the upper part of the avenue, I noticed something that caught my attention. On the one hand, I could see people who looked happy at that moment, enjoying a pleasant chat with family and friends while sipping a cup of coffee. They looked like people with high purchasing power.

In strikingly high contrast, I saw people dressed in rags, with sad, distressed faces, begging for alms in some corners of the street, carrying all their possessions in a small backpack. I also saw wealthy people with worried, dissatisfied, and angry expressions.

A few days later, on the steps in front of a shop, a young woman and a little girl were sitting, both drinking from a glass and sharing a piece of bread. As I walked by, they turned to me and greeted me with big smiles; they looked happy, and their eyes were shining.

Why do some wealthy people, who have everything they want, live frustrated and unhappy, while others in the same condition are happy and enjoy life more? Why do some people live in scarcity and poverty while others achieve everything they set their minds to? What makes some poor people live sad and hopeless lives while others are happy with a cup of coffee and a loaf of bread, sitting on a few steps? The difference lies primarily in their inner self, in their belief system.

LIMITING BELIEFS

Throughout our lives, we form different beliefs about practically everything: cultural, social, religious, family, personal, beliefs about money, other people, or the environment. Every day, these beliefs can be reinforced, modified, or even changed or replaced through our experiences and thoughts about them.

A belief is not necessarily a reality. A small child may firmly believe that his teddy bear is alive and has feelings, but it is not the truth. As we grow up, we tend to form beliefs that we accept without questioning, eventually becoming our reality. Most of these beliefs are unconsciously imposed by our ego, and many of them are negative and unrealistic.

Without exception, every limiting, rigid, negative, irrational belief comes from nothing more and nothing less than the ego. These limiting beliefs are watered and grown by fear and by ignoring many of the things we are learning in this book.

Due to fear, the ego tries to protect itself from external factors and from things that may happen in the future, and it does so by using strong patterns of limiting thoughts and putting up barriers to avoid supposed harm. However, the actual threat lies within yourself, in listening precisely to the voice of the ego in your mind, thinking it is you, and in each of the beliefs that limit you, hinder you, minimize you, and make you feel incapable of improving in any aspect of your life. The real threat is the ego.

Whatever you believe will become your reality. If you live with the idea that you can no longer be happy because the world is in chaos, you will see that everywhere. We cannot stop the events that happen every day around the planet; things like this were happening before you were here, and they will continue to happen afterward. It is crucial to stay informed without being overwhelmed by negative news. Your organism is not designed to remain in a state of constant alert and stress. Fear is not your nature; it is the nature of the ego. The real war you must face and win is first within yourself, against the ego and its army of limiting thoughts, emotions, and beliefs.

The limiting belief that most urgently needs to be replaced in your life is the belief that the voice of the ego in your mind is you. This is a person's most damaging belief because it constantly floods the mind with thoughts of fear, sadness, worry, and anxiety, negative events of the past and stirs up the heart with feelings of insecurity, anger, envy, greed, and guilt.

Sometimes, you may come to think that you have two personalities within you. One is good, positive, forgiving, and loving; the other is negative, fatalistic, resentful, worried, and victimizing. The latter is the ego; it is not you; it is the belief that has taken root and that you have accepted. Your true personality is in your consciousness, in your soul, and in your spirit; your essence is good, happy, kind, forgiving, loving, and is silently crying out to be released from the oppression of the ego.

If you have ever felt that something in your life is holding you back, preventing you from moving forward, sabotaging you, or preventing you from being happy or truly enjoying life, that is nothing more than the system of limiting beliefs implanted by the ego and unconsciously accepted by you.

The ego knows that its dominion and oppression over you ends when you awaken in your spirit and become aware of its negative influence on your mind. Then, you begin to know yourself and discover the magnificent being you really are.

IDENTIFYING LIMITING BELIEFS

Some of the underlying thoughts for several of the limiting beliefs might be, "I'm not good at that, "It sounds too good to be true," "Life is too hard and difficult," "Only a lucky few do well," "I'm not smart enough or good enough or young enough to do that," "Everything goes wrong for me, I can't get it right," "There are no opportunities here," "I get fat just by looking at food," "That disease has been in my family and I will surely have it too," "If I show my feelings they will take advantage of me," "To survive in this life, I must be tough and think only of myself."

These are just a few examples of how to identify self-limiting thoughts. Behind every statement we make, there is a belief, which can be negative or positive.

Any negative belief you have about yourself that makes you feel inferior, inadequate, ignorant, incapable, or too small or too old is put there by the ego and is based on fear and ignorance of who you really are. Your true self does not see a distorted reality; it knows that you were created in the image of the Eternal Creator and that by awakening your consciousness, you can begin to change everything for the better. The transformation in your life depends on you; you have been given the tools to renew yourself; you must do it yourself, and that change begins in your mind.

We must be aware of our thoughts in each area. For example, there is a limiting belief behind thoughts such as, "Money makes people bad," "If I have a lot of money, I will not be spiritual," "Humble people are poor," and "It is bad to want to prosper or want material things," "I do not have opportunities to prosper," "Life is difficult here," "I am satisfied with..." and so on.

The Eternal God says that he wants us to live a life of abundance in all things, and all things also include the material. Money is something external that can have no inner influence but through the ego, which is the one that focuses on the external. In other words, the person with their free will decides whether they allow the ego to rule them and incline them towards greed and presumption or whether they remain in consciousness through the spirit and use their resources for good to live better for themselves and their family and to help others.

Money does not corrupt a person, but it brings out the inclination that the person had before. If the ego controls them, the inclination will be toward the bad and negative, but if the person has a powerful awakening, begins to be guided by the spirit, and becomes conscious, the inclination will be toward the good, healthy, and positive.

Another limiting belief is to think that you are meant to suffer in this life and that you must accept all the negative things that others do to you. For example, a husband who is an alcoholic beats his wife, is unfaithful, and does not provide for his family, and his wife says, "It is the cross I have to bear." Similarly, a manipulative, materialistic, and reckless wife who, instead of building her own home, destroys it herself, and her husband thinks that in order not to create arguments, he has to put up with all the blackmail of the bad woman.

The same thing happens with children who are disobedient and rude, and the mother thinks it is a mother's selflessness and suffering to put up with it. Or, at the other extreme, an overprotective and manipulative mother who wants to control the children, and they have to put up with everything. Neither is the right thing to do. Children should honor and respect their parents, and parents should not provoke their children to anger. The ego provokes inappropriate behaviors and non-functional beliefs that need to be urgently replaced.

Another example of limiting belief is to estimate that the Creator's will is that a person should live in scarcity and poverty and suffer to purify themselves and become more humble or spiritual. That would be the opposite of the nature of all things He created. Nature itself grows, develops, blossoms, and bears fruit. He wants you to be happy, in love, in fullness, and to have everything in abundance so that you can fulfill your purpose and help others because when someone is in need, we must first have in order to give.

What good is it to say to someone who is hungry, go in peace, and I will pray for you, or I would like to help you, but I have nothing to give you? We give what we have; we cannot share with others something that we lack in our own lives, whether it is something material or love, peace, joy, comfort, or forgiveness.

A common limiting belief is when the ego launches mental attacks on a person, making them feel guilty for being happy while others in their family are not. Or it makes them feel selfish for feeling at peace while someone close to them lives tormented in their emotions by their own ego. But you cannot bring joy to others if you are sad, nor can being in a state of poverty and scarcity help others in need.

Sometimes, people just need company or someone to listen to them. To do this, we must first learn to listen to our own true voice and then learn to enjoy our own company.

We don't bring any good to the world, our loved ones, or ourselves by living a sad life just because others are sad or by being poor just because others are poor, nor can we feel guilty for prospering and being emotionally well when other family members haven't had a spiritual awakening yet, on the contrary, by being an example for them we can inspire them to renew their minds and transform themselves, in that way they will also achieve peace, happiness, prosperity and a full life.

REPLACING LIMITING BELIEFS

Every human being wishes to improve in some aspect: in their health, relationships, economy, overcoming the past, living happily, in peace, and feeling loved and useful. Everything has an order. Balance begins when we unmask the voice of the ego in our mind and become conscious. Then, we work on breaking all attachments and continue to identify and replace negative beliefs with new, healthy, and functional beliefs.

A few years ago, I had a limiting belief about time. I was running from one place to another, always hurrying to finish that day's occupations. I used to say that time was passing too fast, that the hours of the day were not enough, and that I was living against the clock. Without realizing it, my focus was on the fact that time was not enough, and without a doubt, that was my reality.

When I began to have an awakening in my spirit and become aware of my thoughts, I was able to recognize this false belief that was preventing me from correcting it. I replaced the previous thoughts with affirmations such as, "I have time for everything, I can do all my occupations in the day and I have plenty of time to do everything I like and enjoy with my family." Surprisingly, the change was almost immediate; I started having time to spare, and it was as if the clock was slowing down, allowing me to do everything I wanted to do and having extra time.

Today I can live relaxed and with more than enough time. What you believe will be. If we believe that there is not enough time, money, health, happiness, or whatever, that will be our reality; if we believe otherwise, things will begin to change. We are governed in our daily lives by our belief system; when it is not right, we have the power to change it.

Your life will always come to where your thoughts are. If external changes are made, but no real change is internalized in the mind, the behavior will return to its old state.

Most people who win a lottery prize enjoy it and feel happy for a while but then return to the same place, ending up unhappy, broke, and in debt, sometimes even more than they were before they won the prize. The limiting beliefs were not replaced, and their lives went back to what they were before in their minds. The reality of each person's life is an exact reflection of their beliefs.

Every limiting belief that we want to eliminate must be replaced by a positive one; this is how our mind works. If the focus is placed on what we don't want, it strengthens and deepens its roots.

The process is very simple; first, the belief that the ego implanted is identified, and then it is replaced with a positive counterpart through focused and conscious thoughts. For example, the limiting belief could be, "I am too old to start studying a career," and the new healthy belief could be, "I can achieve whatever I propose because I am connected through my spirit to the inexhaustible source of power, which is the Eternal God." Other examples include "I don't have enough money, it is not enough." A new positive belief could be, "I have more money every day, and new ideas and opportunities to prosper come to me." "The world is getting worse and worse; it is no longer possible to be at ease." The functional belief could be, "In the world, there are two extremes, but I decide to focus on the good and be happy."

These are just a few examples, but you can adapt them to whatever you want to replace in your life; whether it is an addiction to cigarettes, alcohol, food, or a bad habit, it all involves the same process: replacing the negative and non-functional belief with a new, healthy and functional one.

You do not remove something and leave the space empty because what was removed will return with more strength, or some bad habit or limiting belief will take that place. Nor do you fight against what you don't want because you would only strengthen it anyway. The focus is on what is new and what you want now. You replace the negative with something healthy, positive, and productive.

Perhaps you identify some harmful habit, vice, or addiction with which you have struggled all your life without being able to overcome it; that is because the focus was on what you did not want and ended up getting stronger, and the idea that it was impossible to overcome it deepened.

At birth, we are blank in our belief system; there are no bad sleeping or eating habits, no vices, no addictions, no attachments, and no limiting beliefs; everything is learned and accepted. And everything learned can be unlearned. There is nothing that cannot be changed or replaced for our own good; there is nothing that cannot be overcome. Absolutely everything is possible through the power given to us in the mind to renew ourselves and transform our own lives.

Some beliefs you identify when you become aware of your thoughts may not need to be replaced but only modified or adapted to your current situation.

When we begin to be conscious, our perspective of life and many things changes. As you turn off the ego of the mind, your spirit shows you through awareness the things you have believed about yourself, others, and the world around you that have damaged and limited you. In this state of meditation and self-analysis, you can take advantage of this to replace or modify those beliefs that you are aware of at this moment. A new thought is planted to replace the old one.

The belief in the Eternal Creator seen from the ego will be of apparent religiosity, of fear; the person will try to fulfill requirements, will do things to be seen and approved by people, and will judge and criticize those who do not do the same they do. They receive a false momentary satisfaction in the ego but are neither free nor happy. They live in cognitive dissonance; they speak one thing but do the opposite; they behave one way when they are in public but another way when they are alone.

When the person is grounded in the spirit and is conscious, they stop doing things to be seen; it is no longer a burden but a delight because the ego no longer interferes. You will be able to notice that you have changed from the ego to the spirit because everything is done with love, joy, and flow. This is the clearest sign that we are in the consciousness, in the spirit, things are flowing, and things are no longer done with busyness and exhausting effort; now, everything that is done flows and is enjoyed.

We begin to be more patient; the things that used to irritate and bother us suddenly cease to be so important. We no longer criticize or judge, and we develop self-control. Emotions no longer rule us, but we have control over them because the ego is extinguished, and our true personality emerges. The pride of the ego disappears, and we become humble. Humility beautifies the face; pride repels.

For this change to take root in your brain and be internalized at a subconscious level, you must do it for forty days. It is something simple; it is not complicated, although it may seem so at first. It is just a matter of forming new habits of thought, and by keeping yourself conscious, the work becomes easier. Life becomes simpler, easier, and more enjoyable when the ego is turned off. What had prevented you from making changes in your life in the past was the ego ruling your mind.

THOUGHTS GAIN STRENGTH WHEN WE REPEAT THEM

The more you think about something, the more it strengthens and takes root. Each thought repeated in the mind gains strength until it is internalized and becomes part of the belief system. The more conscious you are of your thoughts and focus on the new thing you want to implement, on what is healthy and positive, the more your new belief system will be strengthened, and the more the limiting beliefs will weaken until they disappear.

It may seem overwhelming at first because we begin to realize that we must renew ourselves in practically every area of our lives; however, everything is gradual. When we plant a tree, we don't expect to harvest fruit the next day, so be patient with yourself, but without being permissive, do not allow the ego to come back and take control of your mind. When the ego is active, your true essence is weakened; therefore, it is as if you stop living so that the ego can live at your expense.

At first, the ego will fight back. It will put thoughts in your mind to discourage you, to make you believe that this will not work for you, that you can't, that maybe you are not doing it right, that it is difficult and tiring, but none of that is true. Go on and believe that you can do it.

Even if you think everything you learn in this book will stay with you during the renewal process, read it as many times as necessary; the more you repeat an idea in your mind, the more it is internalized, and that is where change occurs.

When you learned to drive, it may have seemed very complicated, but with practice, the process was internalized, and now you do it naturally. The same thing happens with the transformation on your mind. With time, this will be a habit that you will do normally and fluidly. It will be your new nature to be inclined toward the good and the positive. Your spirit will be the one that guides you, not the ego.

Believing is the key to everything in life. If your belief system is rigid and limiting, then your life will also be rigid and limited; on the other hand, if your beliefs are healthy, positive, and functional, so will your life. It is a matter of what you choose to believe. According to your faith, it is done. Faith is active, growing, and strengthening with each new thought you choose to have in a focused way. Fix your mind on the change you want, and you will be in the process of transformation.

INNER HEALTH

When the ego recalls a painful memory from the past, it automatically activates an emotion linked to it, and the subconscious mind takes it as something that is happening to you again in the present.

Any mental and emotional suffering you may have at this time from past situations is caused by the ego being active in the mind. When you feed your spirit, your consciousness awakens, and it is there that you are able to recognize the harmful work of the ego. At that moment, you have the power to choose to replace any negative thoughts, and the ego then shuts down—this is where the inner healing process takes place.

You cannot heal by being in the past, which numbs consciousness, nor can you heal by being in the future because you enter into a state of ego-generated self-hypnosis where you visualize negative events that could occur and cause anxiety. You can only heal by being in the present, by being conscious.

Throughout our lives, we have all received hurtful words and negative comments such as, "You can't," "You don't know," "You don't understand," "You're not worth it," and "You're not this or that," and these are labels that we unconsciously accept. These toxic words enter the mind, and the ego takes hold of them and stores them to torment us; each time it brings them to mind, they become stronger and cause more emotional damage.

We end up believing that we are what others think of us. We must make a firm resolution to remain conscious, identify these harmful thoughts, weaken them by replacing them with positive thoughts, and develop a healthy self-concept. You are what God says about you and what you choose to believe about yourself.

When a memory comes to mind, it becomes malleable and fragile; in that moment, you can change it or replace it. Being aware of this fact is one of the most powerful internal healing tools there is. You have the power in your mind to strengthen or weaken anything that harms and hurts you. What makes you suffer in your emotions begins and ends in the mind. If you are aware of a limiting thought, memory, or belief, in that instant, it is malleable and vulnerable; you can replace it or substitute it. You can forgive and let go. This is how we heal inwardly.

There was a young woman who lived tormented by her emotions; she complained all the time about her parents, about not having enough money, about what she had to spend on gas for her car and food for her pet, about her job, about having to clean her room, about her younger brother... in short, her mind was focused on all these negative things.

On one occasion, she had an accident and temporarily lost her memory. After a few days in the hospital, the doctor said she could go home and that her memory would return in a matter of weeks. When her mother came to pick her up at the hospital, the young woman did not recognize her, so she explained that she was her mother and that she had gone to pick her up to take her home. She also told her that her father and younger brother were waiting for her at home, that her cat would probably be happy to see her again, and that when she fully recovered, she would be able to drive and return to work.

The young girl was very excited to know that she had a dad, a mom, a brother, and a kitten. She was so happy to have a family and to know that she had a job, a car, and a house to live in with her own room. Then she exclaimed, "I feel so happy; my life is really perfect!"

When her memory returned, the young woman became more aware of how all her focus was on the negative and that her mind caused her suffering. Things around her continued the same as before. However, she decided to focus on the good, and her life changed.

She chose to be happy and replace negative thoughts with a positive thought pattern, and what happened was a healing process. All inner changes are reflected on the outside.

Life is not meant to suffer, to be sick in emotions and in the body. Life is not about spinning on a hamster wheel, getting nowhere, working to put food on the table, and watching your paycheck go away as soon as you receive it. It is not meant to live in mental torment caused by the ego. It is not meant for you to live numb and with your true essence turned off.

Life should be enjoyed to the fullest, with abundance in every aspect, and should flow freely. For this to be so, we must awaken and take control of the power given to us to generate changes in the mind. Let us always remember that our transformation comes from renewing our minds. This work is personal; you cannot do it for others, nor can others do it for you.

In our world, there is a duality, the two extremes. We do not deny the reality when we go through some difficult circumstances, we are not negligent, but we analyze the situation; we make changes, modifications, and the necessary preparations, but we do not focus on the negative, which increases fear and the power of the ego to influence our minds negatively. Once we have done our part, we deliberately focus on the best possible outcome and enjoy every moment of the present because that is all we really have.

Remember that one of the basic functions of the mind is the power of choice. There are roses in the world as well as thorns; we cannot deny one or the other. However, you can choose to see the roses instead of the thorns, being careful not to thorn yourself. Both are there, flowers and thorns. Each one of us possesses the power to choose our focus, and what we focus on ultimately shapes our experience.

The same process is required to make the decision to laugh or cry, to enjoy or to be bitter, to see the positive or the negative, to see the thorns or the extraordinary beauty of flowers, their vivid colors, and to enjoy their fragrant aroma.

CHAPTER 4

THE BRAIN'S EXTRAORDINARY DESIGN

The human brain is a universe in itself, an extraordinary wonder. In many areas, it remains a mystery even to scientists.

It controls thought processes, emotions, behavior, and speech and coordinates body movements, heart rate, digestion, breathing, and temperature. It contains approximately 86,000 million neurons. It is capable of performing all kinds of complex functions. It is so amazing and powerful that through the mind, positive changes can be made that even science would say are impossible. The mind has no limitations; whatever you can imagine, your brain will immediately follow it to make those mental images your reality.

The brain receives information from the subconscious mind (memories) and through the senses. The brain interprets what you see, hear, feel, speak, and taste and translates it into images that go to the mind. Those mental images are taken as an order, whether you like what you are thinking or not, whether you want it or not, whether it makes you feel good or bad, your brain takes it as an order that it does not question; it simply starts working so that those images in your mind become your life experience.

For this reason, it is extremely important to remain conscious and focus your thoughts on the positive, on what we do want, on the solution, and not on the conflict. Pay attention to the music you listen to or the movies you watch because all this is interpreted in your brain as reality and as a command that this is what you want.

We know that there is duality in life; good and bad things happen, things that we want and things that we don't want, and things that we like and things we don't like. It is precisely this contrast that helps us in the mental process of choice: to appreciate and focus on the things we want and to accept and reject thoughts, information, and memories.

A POWERFUL TRANSMISSION TOWER

Your brain is like a powerful tower that emits frequencies through your thoughts. The power of your focus determines the energy that attracts the things you think about. If you do not pay attention to something, your brain does not focus on it, resulting in no signal being generated and no emotions being activated internally.

If we do not know our design and how we function, we will go through life on autopilot, being ruled by the ego, without knowing how to make profound and true changes that will lead us to a transformed, fulfilling, and prosperous life in every way.

The brain converts every thought into a powerful signal that is launched into your organism, provoking reactions of all kinds. It also sends a signal outward from you, influencing your entire environment. Your thoughts are charged with electromagnetism and attract similar things into your life.

THAT WHICH YOU RESIST IS ATTRACTED WITH GREATER FORCE

The bad, the negative, does not go away by focusing on it or talking about it constantly; on the contrary, by doing so, we are giving it power, and we end up magnifying it because the brain prints the images of those thoughts to attract them to us with more strength.

It's possible that in the past, you may have resisted things that you didn't want. You may have talked and complained about them to others and thought about the negative things constantly. By fighting against what was hindering you, you may have unknowingly given it more power over you. Your brain tends to magnify and give importance to everything that enters your mind. Anything that you resist is strengthened.

The way your brain works in your favor is by putting your focus on what you want. Consciously think about it and visualize it as if it is already a reality. Then, the brain internalizes it, and change happens. In the same way, whether it's an addiction, a relationship, inner growth, self-esteem, social skills, or financial lack, anything you have resisted or struggled with, immediately shift your focus to what you do want instead of thinking and talking about what you want to change or eliminate from your life.

DOING MORE THAN ONE THING AT A TIME AFFECTS BRAIN CAPACITY

Your brain has an impressive capacity, working day and night nonstop to keep you alive and regulate all bodily functions. However, the mind can only be focused on one thing at a time. Contrary to common belief, multitasking is not good for the brain. We are not designed to multitask. What actually happens is that attention is shifted from one thing to another very quickly, always focusing more on one place and neglecting another.

Let's say that by executing several things simultaneously, the brain is overloaded and stops performing its internal functions optimally. On an emotional level, a stress signal is sent, which makes the brain shrink and causes memory impairment, clouds the ability to find appropriate solutions to conflicts, affects emotions, and even causes alterations in metabolism. The person becomes more vulnerable to the judgments and opinions of others. When the brain is under stress, it does not work properly, and reality is perceived in a distorted way.

We live in an accelerated world, and we have become accustomed to wanting everything to be fast and to do several things at the same time to finish our daily occupations; this causes us to live out of real-time, out of the present. Our focus is on everything and nothing. Multitasking affects our brain's ability to perform its functions properly to keep us alive and in balance.

It is necessary to remind ourselves, over and over again, until we internalize it, that practically all the disorder in managing our lives has been caused by believing that the voice of the ego is our own voice. If we remain aware of this, the sense of urgency and running from one place to another disappears, and we can focus on the present.

You have to do your daily activities while enjoying them, focusing on one thing at a time. There will always be things to do, but the key is that you manage your agenda rather than your occupations manage you. Doing things calmly and focusing on each activity we do brings multiple benefits to your physical, mental, and emotional health. Of course, the ego will try to tell you in your mind right now that you have so many things to do, that you can't do them calmly, that your life is like that, or that your job demands it, and so on.

The ego is like a repetitive computer program in all minds. But you, with your free will, are the one who governs your mind. What you choose to believe and focus on will grow.

NEGATIVE THOUGHT PATTERNS CAUSE BRAIN DAMAGE

Negative thoughts cause damage to your brain, causing the entire cellular functioning of your body to go haywire.

There are about one hundred billion cells in the human body, ready to obey any order given to them by the brain through your thoughts. Neither your brain, nor your cells, nor the neurons question what you think; for them, you are the ruler of your organism, and they react and obey immediately to your thoughts.

When your thoughts are negative, chaos ensues that affects your health—you are actually generating brain damage. A negative thought pattern is like an octopus that releases black ink, like a poison that is secreted inside you, produces affectations in every area, and also impacts externally. It leads to depressive and anxious states; both your brain and every cell of your organism go into a state of survival instead of being focused on keeping you in balance and well-being. They are only fighting against the internal chaos provoked by toxic thoughts.

Every single cell in the body is connected to the heart, and the heart is directly connected to the brain, so each and every one of our thoughts literally affects the entire organism. Every cell is altered for better or for worse, depending on the quality of thoughts you have.

Our brain receives proteins through the food we eat, the quality of which depends on the quality of the food we eat. So, what you eat also influences your mental processes.

The instant you become aware that the ego is implanting toxic thoughts into your mind, you can use the tool of asking yourself questions to move into a state of healthy thinking. When you ask a question in your mind, your brain immediately stops everything else to find an answer. Turn it into a positive game by asking questions like, "What is around me that I like?" "What things do I love about life?" "How will I feel when my dreams and goals become a reality in my present?"

THE BRAIN LEARNS FROM MISTAKES

Your brain also learns from mistakes. For example, if you try something for the first time and you don't do it right, your brain registers that fact and learns what to do next time. When we are in our true essence, in consciousness, the brain works better and learns faster because we take mistakes and errors in a positive and mature way. On the contrary, the ego feels hurt when it makes mistakes and immediately loads the soul with guilt; its path leads to damage and affectation in the whole organism and the environment. It clings to things, and even when it sees the damage, it moves toward it because it is foolish, anxious, and puts up a fight.

When we remain in consciousness, the spirit guides us to the good path. We enter into a positive state of alertness to recognize danger and turn away. We learn the art of good thinking and choosing our thoughts.

It is in the brain, with the mind, that you think and make decisions that shape your life, minute by minute. The mind is directed either by the ego (unconsciousness) or by the spirit (consciousness).

The energy of your thoughts produces physical manifestations. They are not just intangible mental processes but have an internal and external impact at cosmic levels.

TURNING OFF THE PREDISPOSITION TO THE NEGATIVE

The mind is so powerful that it can turn off learned emotional patterns and predispositions toward the negative. For instance, moodiness is not something that is inherited but rather learned. However, it can be triggered by accepting external labels such as "you are as grumpy as your father." If that comment is accepted in the mind and is believed, it is activated and stored, predisposing the person to moodiness or impatience. We must be careful what we say to others, especially children and adolescents, but most of all with what we accept in our minds.

What really matters is not so much what others may say or think about you as what you choose to believe about yourself. What you accept as truth in your mind will become your reality.

During the night, while you sleep, the hippocampus—an important part of the brain responsible for learning and memory—processes the information about your thoughts from the day. It identifies which thoughts are important, particularly those that are repetitive or constant, and stores them in your long-term memory. This then becomes part of your belief system, which directs your life in a particular direction, positive or negative, depending on the kind of thoughts you have during the day.

This information is stored in the subconscious throughout your life and later returns to the brain, influencing its processes and functions. The brain always relates the external information you receive with the information stored in your subconscious, activating or deactivating the predisposition towards the negative. Now you understand better why it is so necessary to replace limiting and negative beliefs. Everything in our being is a perfect gear assembly, a miniature universe affected by itself.

THE BRAIN BELIEVES IN EVERYTHING THE MIND DECIDES

If we take two plates of peach-flavored yogurt, but to one of them we add pink artificial coloring and give it to someone to taste, even before tasting it, the person will decide in their mind that the pink yogurt is strawberry-flavored, and the peach-colored one is precisely peach. This is because the mind immediately relates everything to what is stored in the subconscious, and the brain believes without questioning. So, in this case, the pink color is associated with the strawberry flavor, and when the person tastes the pink yogurt, they will say that it tastes like strawberry, although it is actually peach.

If we then blindfold them and give them the yogurts to taste again, they will realize that both yogurts have the same flavor because, without the visual cue of color, they no longer associate the color with the flavor, and then the brain functions correctly without the bias of the mind.

This is just one example to help us better understand how the brain works. The brain relates what we are experiencing in the present with our past experiences, so we are inclined to prejudge, limit, and make decisions automatically as if we were a computer program.

In the process of self-knowledge and awakening to consciousness, the mind is renewed, and we can change the mental programming of the past that has led us to judge, doubt, and fear. All these changes happen naturally when we deliberately focus our attention on the end result, on what is healthy and good.

AUTOMATION

For most of our lives, the mind has been accustomed to taking us where the ego pleases. We have not been aware of the power we have to control what happens in the mind, so at first, it may seem like a lot of work to become aware of our thoughts and direct them toward the healthy and positive; however, each self-directed thought, each new positive thought, will gain weight until it is stored in the subconscious and an automation effect will occur, that is, you will begin to do it naturally and effortlessly, a habit of positive thinking will be created.

Any process of change requires forty days of daily and conscious practice. Then, the mind is inclined toward the good and the positive; it focuses on the solution and not on the conflict, on what you do have and want, and not on what you lack or do not want.

The automation process also works in reverse. When you think and focus on the negative, complaining, victimizing yourself, and so on, your mind leans toward the bad and the toxic. With every thought you build up or tear down your own life, and either the negative automation process of stagnation, loss, and death is strengthened, or the positive automation process of transformation, prosperity, and life is strengthened. The power of choice is yours; your free will will bring about renewal in your mind and transformation in your life.

YOUR BRAIN CAN GET STRONGER WITH AGE

There is no limit to your growth; even if you lived a hundred years longer, you would continue to learn and develop in a continuous process of improvement throughout your life. Previously, it was believed that neurons in the brain were lost and that their capacity weakened with age, but through neurogenesis, we can see that new neurons are constantly being generated.

Let's say that with each night's rest, while you sleep, the brain forms a mass of proteins ready to be used each morning with your thoughts for that day. Those thoughts structure the proteins into brain branches that will shape your existence. Your thoughts shape your brain. The intangible (thoughts) generates something material (proteins and brain branches).

No matter what age you are today, you can have the same learning capacity as before or even better. Your brain has a hitherto unknown capacity; we should not limit it by accommodating ourselves to limiting beliefs about our capacity. The brain truly is impressive. The more we feed the spirit, the more our consciousness awakens, and the wall that we thought was the limit is torn down, revealing a universe beyond with infinite possibilities we never knew existed.

During your awakening process, there will be days when it seems easier to make changes and be conscious, while other days it will be more difficult, or you will suddenly become aware and realize that you had spent some hours immersed in the mind of the ego. Just take back control of your mind, and do not get discouraged; no eagle is born flying; every process takes time, and everything has to be done with joy, without busyness, flowing.

Take moments to rest throughout the day. Rest helps the mind, brain, and muscles recover and strengthen. Meditate on the good, close your eyes, focus on relaxing your body, and take slow, deep breaths. This will help clear the mind and return you to a state of consciousness from which you can guide your thoughts in a healthy way.

You can overcome the shortcomings you may identify in your life right now by consciously choosing to focus on filling them rather than on their lack.

The Creator, the inexhaustible source of all power in the universe, has endowed us with an amazingly wonderful brain and a mind with the power to accomplish incredible things. He put his power in our minds so that we can renew ourselves by using it consciously. How amazing!

CHAPTER 5

THE POWER OF THOUGHTS

THE CONSCIOUS AND SUBCONSCIOUS MIND

I am passionate about this topic: the power of thoughts. First of all, it is important to know that the mind is divided into two parts: the conscious and subconscious mind.

CONSCIOUS MIND

It is the one with which we can reason, see things logically, analyze, and decide which thoughts, ideas, or beliefs to accept and which to discard.

SUBCONSCIOUS MIND

The subconscious mind cannot discern or differentiate between what is real or imagined and what you want or don't want. It does not reject anything you perceive; it receives everything and automatically stores it, creating mental objects that it then sends to you as thoughts. The subconscious mind is so vast that everything is stored in it from the moment you are born. It is like a submerged iceberg of which you can only see a small part.

Nor does it recognize time, such as past, present, and future. It perceives everything in the present. When you remember something from the past, it takes it as a new event happening to you at that moment. If you visualize yourself riding a bicycle in a forest or running, the same process is activated in your brain and in the same sequence as if you were doing it in reality. What you remember, what you live in the present, and what you imagine and visualize of the future are stored in the subconscious in the same way. Therefore, everything a person does in their mind is as if they were doing it in reality.

Has it ever happened to you that the more you think about something painful that happened to you, the more it affects you? Or the more you turn over in your mind something from the future that worries you, the more anguished you become? This is because the subconscious doesn't distinguish between the real, the imagined, or the memories; it's all like a real present experience that gets more significant every time you think about it. Not only that, but everything you think about it takes it as a command and immediately forms mental images related to those thoughts, which it sends back to you in the conscious mind, creating a cycle that influences your thought patterns, emotions, attitudes, words, and decision-making.

While you sleep, your subconscious searches its storage for similar thoughts and brings them back to you as soon as you wake up. If you think too much about something during the day, your subconscious considers it urgent and will even wake you up at midnight to present you with everything it finds in its storage related to it.

As expected, when we are not aware of this fact, we accept whatever the subconscious mind sends us, and so we spend our days in a toxic cycle of upsetting, depressing, and exhausting thoughts that we unconsciously create. If we don't stop it by being conscious and choosing to think what is right, the cycle continues uninterrupted until our thoughts become our life reality.

It is estimated that we have about sixty thousand thoughts daily, of which 95% are influenced by our subconscious mind. When we are not aware of our thoughts and do not filter them but instead accept everything that comes our way, it is our ego that fills the subconscious with the most information. This information is then used against us from within, causing negative, repetitive, and similar unconscious thoughts.

Now, the conscious mind handles 5% of the thoughts we have. Once we have begun the process of having a powerful awakening, we can more clearly identify the ego, attachments, and limiting beliefs and their influence on negative thought patterns and choose healthy thinking.

As we saw before, any negative thought, belief, or limiting idea becomes malleable and fragile the moment you become aware of it. At that moment, you can choose to replace it with a new positive idea or modify it by making adjustments to your belief system. Renewal occurs by being conscious, choosing to think about what helps us, the end result of what we want, and replacing negative thoughts with others that are functional.

EVERY THOUGHT COUNTS

Our life is not built with bricks but with each one of our thoughts. If you remain conscious, your emotions become signals, indicators that show you if you are on the right path or if you have stopped being conscious and the ego has returned to rule your mind.

When you have strong negative feelings, stop, analyze why you have them, and when they started. If you must solve something and take action, do it. Every emotion is triggered by a thought; you will find that usually, when we feel bad, it is the ego using its basic emotions of fear, guilt, anger, and sadness. Listening to the voice of the ego shuts down hope and love, and we enter a cycle of anxiety and stress.

Begin to be a guardian of your own life and prevent the entrance of deficient and destructive thoughts. Above all treasure, guard your heart, your mind, for that is where life emanates. The power to choose what thoughts we allow in our minds is extremely simple and, at the same time, extraordinarily powerful. You have the power to choose life or death, blessing or curse, emotional stability or inner conflict, hatred or forgiveness, prosperity or lack, peace or anxiety. All of these are activated or deactivated in your mind by your thought choices.

We are human beings living in a world in which not everything is pleasant and good, and we all have negative and challenging experiences. We cannot be smiling all the time, just as we cannot live angry and scared all the time. As we have seen, when we face a situation, we deal with it, we analyze the possible solutions, and we do our part, but we do not remain fixed on it, nor do we lose our peace until it is solved because if we do that, our emotional stability will depend on the external circumstances being always fine, and in life, external factors are constantly changing.

Emotional stability and true peace are not found outside, in circumstances or people, but inside each one, in the spirit, and we can reach that state of balance through the conscious mind, feeding the spirit, our true essence.

THOUGHTS CARRY WEIGHT

Just as prayers are cumulative, so thoughts gain strength and accumulate, and each one attracts other similar ones until, so to speak, they gain enough weight and become internalized; they go down into the subconscious mind to be stored.

When you detect an intrusive thought, you have a few seconds to eliminate it and replace it with another healthy thought; that is, you take your attention away from it and focus on something positive. When you don't do this and instead fix your attention on the bad thought, it will immediately bring with it many more of the same kind, trapping your mind in a whirlpool of toxicity.

Thoughts are compelling, triggering internal processes that affect virtually every area of your life.

Every thought triggers an emotional response. If a negative thought remains parked in your mind for too long, it will cause an imbalance in your organism. As we have already mentioned, the greatest suffering in life comes from the ego dominating the mind and tending toward fatalism.

A negative thinking habit always triggers stress, anxiety, depression, guilt, burnout, and illness. It is believed that about 80% of diseases are linked to a toxic thought pattern and constant negative emotions.

There are no genes that predispose a person to depression, anxiety, or addiction. Genes can determine physical characteristics, but they do not affect the thought process or the free will to choose which thoughts are accepted into the mind.

On the contrary, thoughts are so strong that each one of them emits an electromagnetic flux that can activate or deactivate genetic predispositions to diseases—your thoughts even influence your DNA. This is impressive stuff!

The electromagnetic impulse of your thoughts is also released outward into your environment, generating a field of positive or negative energy around you. This energy attracts similar things to you. If your thoughts are healthy, the electromagnetic flow they emit will also be healthy, as will the energy you project, and you will begin to attract the healthy, the good, and the positive. If your thoughts are negative, complaining, stressful, or angry, your entire inner being is in conflict, and the energy around you darkens, attracting people and events that are similar to your own thoughts.

The most difficult part is accepting and understanding that something as simple as choosing thoughts has such power to transform life in every facet. The mind is like a powerful computer program that we have been programming all our lives with every thought, and everything, without exception, can be reprogrammed to obtain the desired results.

YOUR LIFE FOLLOWS THE PATH OF YOUR THOUGHTS

Your life inevitably leads to the place of your thoughts. For your life to change course and be transformed, you must renew the way you think.

Let's say that your mind is a field that is being fiercely

fought over by the ego. When consciousness awakens in the spirit, your true nature takes control of the mind and begins the process of clearing away the debris that the ego has accumulated over the years.

The mind ceases to be a minefield that suddenly explodes without warning and becomes a fertile and productive field.

We have already learned that the subconscious mind does not question or analyze your thoughts; whatever you focus on, regardless of whether you want it or not, will work to get your life to that place. Let's say you hear a heartbreaking song, your subconscious will take it as an experience that happened to you and as something you are looking for in your life reality. If you watch a sad, dramatic, or suspenseful movie, it will also interpret it as a reality that has happened to you and as something you want to keep happening in the future, so it will constantly bombard your mind with thoughts suggesting that you make decisions that lead to it.

In the biblical story of Job, we find a man who was always worried about his children, wondering if they had done something wrong and if their actions would cost them their lives. He had his attention, his focus on those thoughts of fear and anguish. Finally, it happened, and in one day, he lost all his children; then he said, "That which I feared the most has befallen me."

This is a lesson for each one of us. Let us learn and be aware that we are leading our lives to the place of our thoughts, and if these are not what we want, it is imperative to correct them immediately. It is a law; what a person thinks inside is what their life will become and what will happen to them. You are giving power to what you repeatedly think about, and you are commanding that to be your life experience.

I know the case of people who were given the worst medical diagnosis after an accident, that they would never be able to walk or use their hand or arm again. They were even told that their recovery was medically impossible. But these people, first of all, knew the power of the Eternal God and the power he has placed in our minds, so they decided that the strongest voice inside them would be the voice of the spirit, and they turned off the suggestive and fatalistic voice of the ego. They affirmed themselves, trusting that their bodies would follow their thoughts, and they visualized themselves as healthy, doing what they used to do and what the doctors said it was impossible for them to do again.

Of course, they followed the medical indications to the letter. They remained in consciousness to exercise the power of choice over their own thoughts and direct them toward the result they sought, and that result came: What was scientifically impossible became possible.

Nothing is impossible for the subconscious mind. Whatever you can imagine, it accepts and believes as a possible and present reality.

And, of course, we know that always and in all matters, the first and last word is with the Creator.

THE POSSIBILITIES ARE ENDLESS

From the moment you wake up in the morning, you start making decisions. You decide whether to get up right then and there or stay five minutes longer, whether to take time to be thankful for the new day or get up in a hurry. You also decide what clothes to wear, what to have for breakfast, what route to take to work, and so on. All day long, we make decisions both in external situations and in our mental thought processes.

The possibilities are infinite in everything, and we reduce those possibilities to the final decision we make in each aspect. For example, all the food and dishes are there, but we limit that infinity of options to what we choose to eat that day. In the same way, it is with the thoughts we decide to have, the emotions we feel, our reaction to what happens to us during the day, how we relate to other people, to ourselves, to our past, the words we choose to pronounce... A whole universe of possibilities is in front of us in every single thing, and it is reduced to the choices we make.

Your life is the culmination of countless decisions you have made. Before you were aware of all this that you are learning, many of these decisions were likely made automatically and unconsciously, driven by the ego, perhaps believing that the possibilities were limited and that you had little choice, but now you are awakening to a completely different reality.

Perhaps you may think that right now, in some areas, your options are not as wide as you would like them to be. If you don't have enough money right now, you can have it if you decide to think about an abundant life in every area. What you believe in, what you are convinced of, will be your reality of life.

It is not about convincing anyone of anything but about each of us being able to awaken in spirit to consciousness and see the infinite possibilities of something greater, something beyond a life of emotional baggage, guilt, sadness, and worry, something beyond a life that struggles to survive.

Life should not feel like a ship in a stormy sea, constantly battered by strong winds. The Eternal put us here to have life and to have it in abundance. All the possibilities are there, and with every thought, you narrow those possibilities down to what you ultimately choose to believe.

It is easy to understand that your life experiences might not have been exactly as you wished them to be based on what you have learned until now. We are the exact reflection of the quality of our thoughts. It is time to put the will into feeding the spirit to stay in consciousness and take the power of choice in our minds. We can choose which thoughts to accept and which to replace with healthy, self-directed thoughts of goodness and positivity.

When you wake up from a bad dream, you are relieved to know that what seemed so real and terrible was just a nightmare. Things often look more significant, more complex, and scarier in the dark of night. Similarly, the ego makes life seem bad, difficult, and heavy, but then morning comes, and we wake up in consciousness, and things look completely different in the light.

Through the spirit, we can see that we are not powerless to improve our lives; on the contrary, it is our duty to do so. We have been given the power and the tools to transform ourselves by renewing our thinking.

CHAPTER 6

THE CREATIVE ENERGY THAT FILLS THE SPACE

In a cold and remote mountainous area lived a family who had never ventured beyond their small village. Everything they knew, everything familiar to their existence, was there: mountains, pine trees, snow, and a lake that remained frozen during the winter months.

On some occasions, they sat down to imagine what would be beyond the mountains and the snow, but they could not think of anything different from what they knew, so they concluded that, although the world was vast and big, surely everything would be very similar to the place where they lived.

One day, when electricity came to that distant and icy place, they got a television. Excited to see new things on their new device, they sat in front of the fire and watched in wonder at people with other cultures and different ways of dressing and speaking. They flipped from channel to channel, eager to see everything.

One of the channels showed a documentary about beautiful beaches, with radiant sunshine, palm trees, warm waters, and a tropical climate with exotic and rare animals, to which they commented, "No, I don't think there is such a place like that in the world, surely it is an invention of the people who put on these television programs to attract an audience. It is impossible that there is such a beautiful place in the world with so much sun, white sand, and turquoise water. It's crazy, it's impossible, there is no such place."

Similarly, we tend to reject what is new or unknown. The ego enters a state of mental blockage because the familiar is the only acceptable thing for it. The new makes it nervous and it is reluctant to leave its comfort zone. However, the fact that we do not know or believe in something does not mean that it does not exist.

When we awaken to consciousness in the spirit, the limited and rigid world begins to break down, and a vast and beautiful world begins to reveal itself before our eyes. In most cases, what we thought was reality is just an illusion, and what we thought was impossible ends up being reality.

You have to discern all these concepts with consciousness, with the spirit, because in the ego, the mind is limited, narrow, rigid, and skeptical. It is blocked to the new, to the good, because it is running in a toxic pattern, clinging to the known, even when the known is harmful. Therefore, the ego is incapable of discerning profound things; it classifies them as madness in order to continue to rule the mind and not be dethroned.

CREATIVE ENERGY

In general, we might think that the invisible space between one thing and another is only filled with air and imperceptible particles. But in reality, nothing is empty. Everything is filled and composed of energy. In every place that seems empty to you, there is energy, both in the room or in the place where you are right now and in every place where you might think there is only air, in every city, in every country, in every corner of this planet, and even outside of it.

There are no empty spaces between one planet and another, between one galaxy and another. Everything is filled and composed of the same energy—a substance that is responsible for creating every single thing in existence, including your body, the trees, the flowers, the animals, the chair you are sitting on, the book you are holding in your hand, or the electronic device in front of you. Everything is made of energy.

Whether we understand it well or not, this energy is a real power. It does not matter if we do not know the scientific or spiritual factors behind it; the important thing is to wake up and know that it is there and that it is always acting in our favor or against us, whether we are aware of it or not.

This energy is like water, and your thoughts are like seeds that, when they come in contact with this creative power, are activated; the seed opens and produces life. The manifestation of what you thought is created and becomes your reality of life. You are living the life you have been activating through your mind by coming in contact with the creative energy surrounding you.

We saw earlier that a thought has the capacity to build proteins in the brain. The thought that is invisible energy gives rise to matter, to something visible. The Creator of the universe made everything with his word, with his creative energy that fills all space.

All your thoughts come in contact with that energy, and this contact produces some changes within you and in the physical world. We were given an extraordinary power in our mind with our thoughts so that we can produce changes in ourselves and the world around us through them.

If our thoughts are healthy, we are building; if, on the contrary, they are negative and toxic, we are destroying our minds, our bodies, and our environment.

ENERGY BRINGS US TOGETHER

The entanglement law of quantum physics has not yet been able to explain how two particles that are miles apart from each other are connected at the same time. Well, there are no empty spaces, so somehow, we are all interconnected through that energy. So what you think and what you do not only has an effect on yourself, but it also affects others.

If most of the people you relate to have a positive thought pattern, the environment will be good, and you will feel comfortable energy around you. When people have a culture and a habit of negative, unhealthy thinking, the environment changes. For this reason, we can find houses, places, and even cities or countries where the energy feels heavy, and there is an atmosphere of oppression and uneasiness.

Each one of us exudes a certain kind of energy that contributes to either a positive or negative environment. If the mind is guided by the ego, the quality of the thoughts will be harmful, and the energy emanating will also be harmful. The person will be at a low level of energy in which true life cannot flourish, blessings stop, and great things cannot flow into that life because the energy is not at the right, healthy, positive, and high level it should be.

When we emit negative energy, we create an environment overloaded with negativity where things don't flow; things break down, there is incident after incident, arguments, nothing goes right, or nothing good remains. It is all an overloaded environment of negativity that the person is creating unconsciously, and that could change instantly by waking up, moving from the ego to the spirit, and starting in the conscious work of choosing thoughts and not allowing just any idea to be camped in the mind. In this way, the energy you emit changes, and you begin to have a flowing life you enjoy.

We continue to work, to put in the will to do what is right, to fulfill our daily occupations, but we no longer go through life fighting and trying to force things to happen. Your focus is on inner work, then when you transform yourself and move from the ego to the spirit, blessings follow you and reach you every day of your life. It is as simple as that. You renew your mind, and your life is transformed in every way.

The perspective of a landscape will never be the same for a little worm moving on the ground at a low level (the ego) as it is for an eagle (the spirit) soaring high and seeing the whole panorama. The worries, efforts, and stress are many when we are far from the spirit because the ego does not know how to rest. It is in your true self, in your consciousness, in your spirit that you find rest, that your perspective on life expands, that you see solutions and blessings, and that you begin to actually live.

It is so natural and so simple. Around you, there is a magnetic field that attracts everything that resembles the energy you are emitting. If you feel afraid, sad, disappointed, or angry, you will attract people and circumstances of the same nature that will increase those feelings and load the magnetic field of your environment with more negativism.

As you move forward in the process of awakening and inner healing, you become more aware of what is happening in your mind, in your emotions, and around you. This allows you to choose thoughts that make you feel good, and as a result, your magnetic field is purified, and you radiate positive energy, drawing positive things toward you.

WHAT IS THE SOURCE OF CREATIVE ENERGY?

The Eternal God is that creative energy that fills the entire universe and extends beyond all that is known. He is the invisible force whose power makes the invisible; He fills everything, every corner, and every space. Everything is created through him, and it has pleased him to put some of that power, that energy, in us so that we can transform our lives through our thoughts. Every moment you think, you create your reality of life. There is power in your mind, and you are responsible for using it correctly.

It does not mean that when we think negatively, we distort the energy, which is the essence of the Creator, but that because we live in a world with two poles, with a duality, we go from being in the positive and healthy pole to being in the negative and toxic pole, generating alterations in the environment and within ourselves.

If you constantly focus on what you lack, your problems, and bad relationships, that the world is all bad, that you can no longer be happy at this moment; if you live in fear, worry, and always think that you have to struggle and suffer, or worse, that you must endure misery and suffering to be a better person in the eyes of the Eternal, then you are mistaken. With this, you are only creating your own environment and reality of life.

On one occasion, a beautiful bird with colorful plumage was flying majestically through the forest; she was a very enthusiastic and positive bird; she lived very happily and was always focused on enjoying her present. While she was enjoying her surroundings, a little worm of a dull and very unattractive color appeared in front of her and moved away a little bit scared and with an angry expression. It was a little worm that spent most of his time being afraid, worried, and angry because of all the difficulties he had to go through in his life.

The bird asked him why he had such a pernicious look on his face. Then the little worm told her that the pond in the forest showed its face to anyone who looked into it but that the pond was so ugly and grumpy that it had frightened him with its angry countenance.

The bird, a bit curious, wanted to investigate, and when she looked into the pond, she saw a beautiful image, bright colors, and a smiling face. Surprised by what the bird said she saw, the little worm peeked out again, and when he did, they both realized that each was seeing their own reflection. The pond was only returning to them what they were projecting. Such is life; such is our mind, and such is the powerful energy that surrounds us.

We perceive the world according to what we are inside. With our beliefs, we make judgments and label what surrounds us, forming our own reality. If the reflection you see in the pond of your life is not what you want, you can change it by being aware of what you are projecting with your mind.

Your thoughts and emotions are energy that is creating and will bring back into your life events, relationships, things, experiences, and people that are assimilated into what you think and feel.

NOTHING IS NEUTRAL, NOTHING REMAINS STATIC

As we already know, nature is always moving forward. Nothing stays the same; it goes forward or backward, and it grows or shrinks. A seed grows into a huge oak or palm tree. Even inanimate things, such as a chair or a house, deteriorate over time. The planets and galaxies, the sun, and everything around us and within us are in a constant process of transformation.

Each of your thoughts and emotions releases a torrent of energy, charged with electromagnetic waves that will return to you what you threw; it is a law. Your life is not an accumulation of isolated events that happen randomly without you being able to do anything about it. Instead, it is a mirror that gives you back the exact reflection of what you put in front of it, and you have the power to change it.

Thoughts affect matter through the creative energy that transforms them into realities, into the life experiences we have every day.

No matter what your past life has been like, your thought pattern, or your belief system, no matter how old you are or how difficult it may seem to you right now to completely transform your life, I want to assure you that if you really want it, you can do it.

If you have lived all your life in an icy place where a paradisiacal beach with palm trees, sun, and white sand seems impossible to believe, the reality is that they do exist and they are there. You just have to open yourself to the infinite possibilities and not limit your decision by choosing what holds you back and keeps you from moving forward; you can begin to choose to believe in the good, to put your will to renew your mind, and to use the tools you have learned up to this point to begin a renewal of your entire existence.

CHAPTER 7

BUILDING A NEW LIFE

Once upon a time, in a beautiful garden, there were two caterpillars, almost identical in appearance but very different on the inside. One prepared every day to advance in her transformation and become a butterfly. She imagined and talked about what she would do when she had wings, the different places she would have the pleasure of visiting, the perfume of the flowers, and the incredible panoramic view she would surely be able to see from above.

The other caterpillar always lived in fear and bitterness; she felt guilty about everything and blamed everyone and everything for the difficult life she had had to live. She complained all the time, and when the enthusiastic caterpillar talked to her about how wonderful it would be when they had wings and became butterflies, she got upset and told her that she had to be realistic, that life was not about dreaming and being positive all the time, that most likely some bird would eat them before they finished their process, or that because of someone else's fault that metamorphosis might not come to a happy ending, because the world was horrible and difficult, that she should only work and work to eat and that she should leave her fantasies behind.

When the time came, because there is no deadline that is not met, no date that does not arrive, the caterpillars began their chrysalis process, in which they would spend about fifteen days before becoming butterflies. During this time of transformation, they began to undergo an incredible metamorphosis. The enthusiastic caterpillar was happy, and although the process was not easy, her eyes were set on the end result; she focused on the magnificent wings she would have, and she visualized herself doing everything she had dreamed of.

The bitter caterpillar was afraid that some animal would devour her while she remained in the chrysalis; she thought it would have been better to stay on the ground as a caterpillar, where she felt safer. She resented the fact that no one tried to ask how she was doing or if they could help her with her metamorphosis.

She kept telling herself that she couldn't do it alone and was frustrated to think of all the friends she had helped throughout her life as a caterpillar, and now none of them were there. She felt like a helpless victim and reaffirmed herself over and over in her mind that she was right to be and think that way and that everyone else was wrong, mean, and ungrateful.

On the last day of their metamorphosis, the chrysalis became crystalline, and the beautiful wings of both appeared. It was time to use their energy to strengthen their wings and break the chrysalis. The bitter butterfly failed to emerge. She felt increasingly frustrated and victimized by everything. Her energy was used to focus on the bad and blame others instead of using it to strengthen her wings and break the chrysalis. Her metamorphosis, as she herself had believed and declared, was not completed.

On the other hand, the enthusiastic butterfly began to move inside the chrysalis to break it with its wings, which was not easy. With each movement, she strengthened her wings and thus completed her amazing metamorphosis. She got tired, and she felt exhausted in an instant, but her desire to fly, to be transformed, was stronger than everything else. Her gaze was fixed on what she wanted, and she was sure this was her life's purpose.

Finally, she made it. The chrysalis broke, and her beautiful orange wings opened majestically. She became a beautiful monarch butterfly. She was ready to start her new life; she had been renewed.

First, it was time to reproduce, and then to fly seventy-five miles a day, to travel the almost two thousand five hundred miles from Canada to the center of Mexico to hibernate. She felt whole and happy, as if she had awakened from a long black-and-white dream to a new life of beautiful and dazzling colors.

If we compare our lives to this story I wrote, we would all probably want to be like the enthusiastic butterfly that transformed herself and achieved her purpose and dreams. However, deep down, many, many people live like the caterpillar that was ruled by guilt, resentment, and fear, as if one difficulty after another is thrown at them every day, and their job is just to dodge and shake off the bad that comes their way, feeling powerless to make a difference.

It is perfectly possible to have the life you want. You can, and it is your responsibility to have a complete metamorphosis.

WE ARE NOT VICTIMS, WE ARE RESPONSIBLE

Many people live their lives as mere spectators, believing that the events happening around them occur randomly and that they are powerless to influence them. They hold themselves accountable for the negative choices they have made in the past, and at the same time, they blame others for their decisions or for the harm inflicted upon them by those around them. This generates a cycle of bitterness, insecurity, and fear that paralyzes the person, clouding their understanding and preventing them from seeing a real way out of many of the circumstances they face. Emotional exhaustion appears and people end up existing in a life of monotony, silently crying out to be released from themselves.

We cannot avoid many of the circumstances that happen to us; we can neither change the past nor the harm that others have done to us. But what we can do is take responsibility for our present lives. As we have seen in the previous chapters, it is very important to wake up and be conscious, to stop believing that the negative voice of the ego in the mind is you. Release all attachments and forgiveness and work in a focused way on thoughts to replace limiting beliefs, including seeing ourselves as powerless victims to renew our lives.

When we victimize ourselves, we send a message to the subconscious mind that others are responsible for our bitterness, fear, insecurity, misery, or whatever negative things we are involved in. The subconscious then blocks itself from finding solutions and constantly reinforces the idea that we are and live this way because of other people, the past, or circumstances.

All this paralyzes and stagnates us. It induces hopelessness and develops an attitude of distrust and suspicion toward everything, judging and criticizing. By victimizing oneself, the soul lives oppressed. Instead of using the energy to strengthen the wings (awakening the consciousness by feeding the spirit) and break the chrysalis, the subconscious undermines the ability to be happy, and the energy escapes, focusing on the bad things in life and attracting more internal and external conflicts.

This may be difficult to accept at first, but on many occasions, the person clings to the feeling of victimization—primarily because the ego is in control of the mind at that moment. They go over and over again the harmful and painful events they have suffered since childhood, they argue with people in their minds, they complain, they get upset, they suffer, and the idea that they are victims before life and before everyone else is reaffirmed. At times, they forgive and let go, but the ego returns with the same suitcase loaded with victimization and anger, and if they are not conscious, they fall back into the same toxic cycle.

Feeling victimized may be more comfortable for the ego because it allows the person to avoid taking responsibility for their own actions and choices while focusing on blaming others and thus avoiding the effort to make changes in their own lives. They keep repeating phrases such as, "I am this way because of what was done to me, because of what happened to me, because I was not taught, I am this way to protect myself."

To remember the negative is to stop living in the present, which is the only real thing we have, and we start living in a non-existent time.

Unconsciously, people think that forgiving and letting go are the same as justifying or agreeing with the other person, but we have already seen that they are not. To forgive is to cut the tie that binds us to the aggressor. It is to stop carrying them everywhere in our minds and emotions. It is to stop releasing poison that does not hurt anyone else but the person who hasn't forgiven. To forgive is to give love to yourself and to have compassion toward yourself.

By victimizing ourselves for the past, we end up being victims of ourselves because we are limiting and self-sabotaging ourselves. We are robbing ourselves of the full and happy life we could have because we choose to focus on the negative things that others have done to us or the bad things that have happened. It is like giving the ego the reins of the mind.

If we go through life unconsciously, we can only live in victimization. In the moment of awakening, we can clearly see that the present is in our hands and not in the hands of the ego, our afflictions, or past difficulties. We understand that we can overcome all the mental and emotional struggles by consciously taking control of the mind, for there is where most of the suffering happens.

If you wait for the past to change or if you focus on people and circumstances to escape victimization and be happy, you will be building castles in the air. The work, as we have already said, is internal. It is work that no one else can do for you, nor can you do for others. When you change, everything around you improves. Life ceases to be black and white, revealing a universe of bright colors.

A MAGNIFYING GLASS OR MIRROR

Choosing not to be a victim does not mean justifying or minimizing the negative things that others have done to us or the bad things we have experienced in life. We have all, at some point, been both victims and victimizers; if you focus on what happened in the past, the circumstances, or what people are doing in the present, you create the expectation of waiting for that to change in order to be happy. Your happiness depends on your change, on stopping listening to the voice of the ego, believing that it is yours, and being conscious.

Usually, the person does not realize that they are victimizing themselves, that although they have suffered some harm from others, the greatest damage is being caused by themselves.

The way you treat yourself will affect the way others treat you. If you feel self-rejection, you unconsciously develop harmful habits that cause other people to reject you. If you feel helpless and unable to change your life, you will attract situations where you feel victimized and powerless.

Your focus should be on yourself to change, not on people or circumstances. Do not spend energy detecting the mistakes of others or judging or criticizing them, even if you think you are right to do so. In the end, you are hurting yourself; you are listening to the ego and turning off your consciousness. The ego brings only chaos and unhappiness. Working with the spirit and awakening the consciousness brings joy, life, and peace.

Victimization, of course, involves blaming others, and blame unconsciously demands punishment. It demands that the other person pay a price. If the offender is nearby, the ego will induce the person to constantly look for any opportunity to attack to make the other feel bad. In victimization, the ego enjoys it when the other suffers because it feels that, in this way, it is paying the price it demands. However, the consequence of this behavior is internal poisoning. The roots of bitterness grow deeper and deeper, and the person cannot be happy nor free.

In its fatalistic perspective, the ego will always find a thousand reasons why you cannot be well. It will give you a huge list of things to be worried about, anxious about, resentful about, angry about, and frustrated about, and this causes a considerable energy drain; it is like going through life with a magnifying glass in your hand, finding what is wrong and detecting what others are doing wrong.

When the spirit awakens, you change the magnifying glass for a mirror and focus your attention on yourself so that the energy that was escaping before is directed towards your own transformation. This is changing from victimization to responsibility. The veil that has prevented you from seeing clearly falls away, and you perceive the thousand reasons you have to be grateful and happy. You experience a calm in your soul.

SELF-JUSTIFICATION

Victimization leads to extreme self-justification; that is, as the person blames and holds others responsible for their emotional turmoil, suffering, bad choices, and so on, their feelings of victimization become deeper and deeper.

They convince themselves that they are right in everything and that everyone around them is wrong. They think they can judge and criticize, and this behavior strengthens their ego.

They are constantly looking for reasons to feel offended, to complain about things, because others do not greet them, or because they did not call them or answer the phone, or because they did not help them or do not visit them. This is a vicious cycle in which offenses accumulate, and that weight sinks them deeper into the mire of victimization.

When you feel that everyone mistreats you or does not give back to you as much as you do in their lives, you should do some self-analysis. We all like to interact with someone who says positive things, adds something positive, listens to us, teaches us, and contributes something good. By nature, we tend to move away from people who complain about everything, who judge and criticize, who speak ill of others and are negative, and who talk only about the bad things that happen in the world or fatalistic things that burden us and rob us our energy.

We are good at detecting negative people, but what if we ourselves are a negative person to others? It is necessary to analyze and correct. When the ego is shut down, and the person stops justifying themselves, then the decision can be made to forgive, to let go, and to take responsibility for their own well-being.

RESPONSIBILITY GIVES YOU WINGS TO FLY

The responsibility to be happy is yours. It does not depend on someone else; it depends on what you choose to think and feel, on your reaction to what happens, and on the inner work you do. You cannot answer for what others think, feel, or do; however, you are fully responsible for how you choose to live your own life. The negative actions of others do not justify a negative reaction on your part. Everyone will be accountable for themselves.

To be responsible, we must first be conscious. Your will must be set on living in inner peace, and no one can work it out for you. Many factors can influence and change the external world at any time, but the inner world is personal work that depends on being conscious of making the right decisions in the way you think.

Respect must be added to responsibility to advance our own well-being. We cannot force others to behave as we consider appropriate. Each person is fighting their own ego, and we are all at a different stage in the process, each at their own pace.

We cannot force them to look for us, to call us, or help us in any way or feel offended and victimized because they do not do so. We must be respectful. Whoever wants to be in your life and bring you something good is welcome; whoever doesn't want to be there is all right. Fortunately, your emotional well-being depends on you and not on others; it depends on turning off the ego and awakening your spirit, which is your personal work.

When we stop seeing ourselves as victims and take responsibility for building our own lives, we start to find solutions where none seemed to exist before. What used to hurt you and make you uneasy will no longer have that effect. You will no longer take things personally or assume that everyone is out to harm or conspire against you because you will be focused on your own well-being. The mental noise will dissipate and you will enjoy more of your own company, of being alone and in silence.

You were given the power to transform yourself. Life is not a matter of luck; it is a matter of being conscious and responsible for our own inner well-being, of knowing ourselves and the one who designed us, of putting your will and making the decision to build the life you want.

You must know with absolute certainty that you will never be faced with a circumstance beyond your power to solve but that with every trial, the power to overcome it comes to your consciousness through the spirit, and even more so when you are connected to the Creator.

TODAY IS THE TIME TO BUILD A NEW LIFE

Start making the right decisions to lead your life toward what you want. Look for opportunities so that you can dedicate yourself to what you love, to something that makes you vibrate, that makes you feel like you are flowing, and not like it is an almost unbearable burden just to get money to survive. Feeling frustrated with your job will also reinforce the feeling of victimization and dissatisfaction.

You may not be able to stop what you are doing right now and start doing what you like because you have bills to pay and a family to support. However, you can start making certain changes and small decisions that will open the doors to what you really want to do.

As I always mention, life is about faith; what you believe will become your reality. If you believe that you can grow your wings and fly, then so be it; if you believe that you will remain locked in a chrysalis and that you can't do anything because life is horrible and torturous and everyone is responsible for your misfortune, then it will be like that. It is up to you to believe in what is right; fix your mind on what is good, the solution, what is pure, and what you want.

Your job is to remain aware to catch any intrusive and harmful thoughts that arise against your well-being and the new nature of the life you are building. Remember that by being aware of any memories or thoughts of victimization, they become vulnerable and malleable, and you can modify them, choosing to forgive, to let go, and to take responsibility for your present balance.

You don't need extra time to work on renewing your mind. You are always thinking; it's just putting your will into being conscious, and that is easier when you feed your spirit.

Sometimes, one of the hardest parts of the process can be living with someone who has not yet begun their renovation. Therefore, it is very important that you share with the people around you what you are learning here so that everyone can move in the same direction. If everyone rows in different directions, progress will be slow and tiring. It is exhausting to move forward when someone is pulling you backward.

However, your attention must be on your own process and keeping the ego out so that it no longer governs you. One ego can never tolerate another; where there are two or more people with their ego dominating their minds, there will always be arguments, envy, and quarrels.

Once you have shared what you are learning with them, allow each one to advance at their own pace without forcing or helping them break out of their chrysalis. Allow them to read and apply what I share in this book. Everything takes a specific time and requires patience, which is another fruit of nurturing the spirit.

It takes less effort and energy to focus on changing yourself than it does to try to change others or get them to understand you. Focusing on others can be exhausting and frustrating. Your responsibility is to work on your own metamorphosis.

If someone had opened the chrysalis of the caterpillar that lived victimizing herself to help her come out, the only thing that would have happened is that she would have died immediately. This is because this process is not external, it is not someone else's work, it is an internal work, and it depends on the butterfly in the chrysalis. With each effort that a butterfly makes to break the chrysalis, its wings get stronger, and it can then break its old life and start a new one.

It is enough to have lived in the past with emotional whirlwinds, mental anguish, lack, resentment, and scarcity, in ignorance of who we are, how we function, and the incredible power entrusted to us to renew ourselves through the mind. We have the free will to choose. You can decide right now if your life will continue in the same way as it is today, or you can choose to start building your new life. You can choose to be happy and have inner peace. You are responsible for it.

The kind of life you live is the sum of the mostly unconscious choices you have made, but all that can change with a single, firm decision in your spirit to stay in consciousness and take responsibility for your present well-being.

CHAPTER 8
THE POWERFUL LAW OF COMPENSATION

SOWING AND REAPING

The entire universe is governed by exact laws that have been established since its creation. They cannot fail, just as the law of gravity always acts on you and everything around you. It is an invisible force that keeps you in the seat where you are now and keeps the seat on the ground without it beginning to rise into the air. Nothing and no one has ever suddenly shot off the planet because the law of gravity has failed. In the same way, every law by which the universe subsists is accurate.

In this chapter, I want to focus on one of those very powerful laws: the law of compensation, cause and effect, or the law of attraction. Here, we will refer to it as the law of sowing and reaping.

Like the law of gravity, the law of sowing and reaping has never failed and never will fail. If you sow a tomato seed, a tomato plant will grow; if you sow a lemon, that will grow; or if you sow an apple seed, you will have a beautiful apple tree.

This law is so common that we have become accustomed to it without a moment's hesitation. No one has ever planted an apple orchard and gone home distressed, worrying and doubting that if this law fails, onions might grow instead of apples. We trust what we know. Even if we don't understand exactly how it works, we don't go out on the street scared that the law of gravity might fail and suddenly send us flying. Whether we understand it well or not, whether we believe in these infallible laws or not, it does not change them; they will continue to work with perfection and accuracy.

EVERY MOMENT YOU SOW SEEDS

The law of sowing and reaping operates not only in the

planted seeds so that each one bears fruit according to its kind. This law is active in absolutely every area of your life. Every thought is a seed that bears fruit. All day long, you are sowing seeds with your thoughts, with what you feel, with every word you say, when you smile, when you encourage someone, when you help, you are sowing seeds in that person, but also in yourself because whatever you give will be returned to you. When you have feelings of indifference, impatience, or anger, you are sowing a bad seed, and with it, you attract similar things to yourself.

A thought activates an emotion, and that emotion activates a feeling. Then, a reaction is produced in your decisions and actions, which in turn produce new, similar thoughts, and the cycle continues, not only internally or in your environment but even beyond. Every action produces a consequence that has repercussions in your present and future life.

 This process of sowing and reaping affects every area of your life, including your relationships, your eating habits, your exercise habits, your hygiene, your rest, your work, your economy, your perception of yourself and the world around you, and your relationships on an internal level, in your soul and your spirit. It is active at all times. You are always sowing something that will bear fruit.

There are only two kinds of seeds: good or bad; there are no neutral or sterile seeds in the fertile field of your mind. Everything we think, speak, feel, and do will produce some fruit according to its kind. If the seed is good, it will produce blessings, but if it is bad, it will bring bad fruit, destruction, loss, destructive emotions and relationships, scarcity, curses, and despair.

We have learned that it is by being conscious from the spirit that we can choose the right kind of seed to plant in the mind. Remember that your subconscious does not know how to discern whether what you are thinking is good or bad for you or whether you want it or not, but every thought produces an image that takes as an order and immediately begins to water it so that it will bear fruit in your life.

Your thoughts are also projected outward, and the creative energy—which is like water that makes the seed germinate—receives that signal that you are projecting out so that your environment becomes the reflection of your thoughts. What you constantly think you are nurturing and it will end up being your life experience. It cannot fail; it is an exact law. With your mind, you start the sowing process, and you nurture and strengthen it with your feelings, words, and actions.

Do you like the way your life is right now? Are you happy with the direction your life is taking in each area? Are there things you would like to improve or change? If you have already put your will into moving forward in the process of awakening, feeding your spirit, and being conscious, you will see that the quality of life you have had until today is equal to the quality of your thoughts, of the seeds you have been planting in your mind.

OUR LIFE ITSELF IS A SEED

A seed can spend many years in a state of waiting as if it were sleeping. All its potential is within it, but it will never bear fruit if it is not planted. That immense potential within it will not be tapped; it will remain in a state of waiting. Our lives are like seeds that have remained in a state of lethargy for many years, lulled to sleep by the voice of the ego without knowing or recognizing who we really are.

The seed is planted when we have a powerful awakening and consciousness is activated. Then, we begin to germinate, to be nourished, to make our way upward to sprout and grow, in a wonderful process that will continue for the rest of our lives until we become a strong tree planted next to streams of water (nourishing the spirit) that will bear abundant fruit.

No tree, flower, or plant grows with frustration, busyness, worry, or trying too hard; it does so effortlessly and fluidly, as it is its nature. At the other extreme, the nature of the ego is to struggle, fight, compete, see the negative, and become tired and emotionally exhausted. Always remember that your true nature, your essence, and what you really are is not the ego. You are the conscious part in your soul that is guided by your spirit, and this nature does not go through life suffering or in fear or anxiety but flows, enjoys, is enthusiastic, always hopes and believes in the best, and always sows good seeds.

The ego must be turned off at all costs; only then can you flow, be free, and live happily. This change does not happen from one hour to the next; it requires the focus of your will to renew your mind, and so you spontaneously transform. You stop being asleep and begin to germinate and grow.

We apply the law of sowing and reaping in everything we do, in our interactions with others, in giving a greeting, a smile, a hug, and everything is returned to us at some point. Have you ever met someone who gives you a half-hearted hug or smile? We should never settle for something half-heartedly, neither in what we give, nor in what we receive, nor in who we are, nor in what we do, nor in what we want in life. To settle with something less when we can go for the best is not sowing the good seed. Your very spirit drives you to sow the good in absolutely everything.

THE INTENTION COUNTS

The intention with which you do things is fundamental because it determines the quality of the seed you are planting. If someone asks you for a favor and you do it, on the surface with happiness and willingness, but inside you have angry feelings or you do it out of obligation, then you are planting a bad seed, and what you will get back will be negative experiences.

Nothing should be done with envy, greed, anger, or to cause harm to anyone. Whatever you do for others, you do for yourself. Even if you think the other person deserves bad treatment from you, according to the law of sowing and reaping, it is what you do that counts, not what others do. It brings back into your life what you do, whether you have a reason to misbehave or not.

That is why, before reaching this point, we have worked on letting go and forgiving and changing non-functional beliefs so that we can sow good seeds from now on. The Creator says that He will give to everyone according to their works and the intentions of their hearts. Leave in his hands the negative things that others may do to you and focus on being aware that you cannot stop the process of sowing; you are doing it all the time, and we are wise when we sow to edify and bless our own lives.

Let us be careful not to speak negatively about others. Even when we consider that we are right, what we sow by speaking, whether good or bad or right or wrong, will be returned to our lives. It is better to speak only what is necessary when the situation warrants it and be fully aware that we are always sowing.

It is wise to develop the habit of not answering questions that have not been asked of us, not giving opinions that have not been asked of us, not asking questions about things that do not concern us, and not giving explanations to those to whom we do not have to give them. The Book of Proverbs says that even a foolish person can be considered wise when they keep silent. And also that a fool (the ego) speaks their mind without restraint, but the wise person (the spirit, the conscience) considers everything they say; that is, they think before speaking.

By being in consciousness, we take care of each one of our thoughts, words, and intentions. On the contrary, people who remain in the ego are not careful about what they say. They overstep the boundaries of respect with reckless and invasive questions, deliberately distorting information they then divulge with bad intentions. They do not realize that with something that seems harmless to them, they are affecting themselves because they are sowing bad seeds, distorting their own environment, and, ultimately, attracting a negative harvest into their own lives.

PAY ATTENTION TO THE SIGNS

Be open to paying attention to what happens in your daily life. If you experience some unwanted incident every day, such as losing your keys, getting extra charges, having things break down frequently, bumping into a chair or hitting a drawer, or having a generally bad mood, these are all signs, reminders to come back to consciousness and change the kind of seed you are sowing and the attitude with which you are doing everything.

The law of compensation is exact; what you sow, you reap. Circumstances may present themselves differently, but they will always be in accordance with the seed you planted. Maybe you get a last-minute cancellation and get upset because you already had your agenda organized, so you take the wrong attitude and act rude or impatient. Days later, you get a flat tire, or your electricity bill comes in higher than usual, or you are treated rudely somewhere; at the moment, you may not see the relationship, but it is the harvest of what you planted days before; everything is like that.

As you awaken more to your level of consciousness, you will be surprised at how you begin to see this relationship in everything that happens in your life. The more you are aware of it, the more opportunities you have to change it until the balance is always tipped in your favor, and you receive more good things every day.

Always take time to attend to your emotions. When you feel sad, angry, or worried, don't ignore it. Some thought triggered those emotions, and you must correct it. Take ten or twenty minutes to live that emotion, to bring to mind what caused you to feel that way. The thought becomes malleable, and you can work with it to eliminate or modify it; if you don't, it will come back later. Every emotional imbalance will cause you to have a negative attitude toward life, and you will sow what you do not want and attract more negative things.

WHAT YOU THINK WILL BE

Life is about believing. Every moment, you are making decisions about what you choose to believe. You believe that you can do something, or you believe that you can't, and what you believe becomes your life experience. With each of these choices you make, you are planting seeds that will inevitably bear fruit.

This does not mean that the things you have to take care of and solve disappear because you believe they are not there. Of course we have to be responsible and take care of our business, but with the firm belief that everything is for the best, that every situation we face will be resolved in the best way for everyone involved, and with our eyes not set on the conflict, but on the solution, without losing peace and emotional stability while solving any problem.

What each person thinks in their mind so is their life. Let us be aware that each constant thought generates weight until it becomes a belief. The more you think about something, the more it becomes embedded in the belief system that governs your life.

When we are conscious, we stop believing what our ego suggests, we are no longer focused on the negative, nor do we incline toward fatalism, fear disappears, and the feeling that something terrible is going to happen goes away; now we develop an expectation that good things are going to happen to us every day, we expect blessings and trust that things are going to turn out well, that we can, we consciously choose to believe and focus on the good.

ALONG THE WATER CURRENTS

We need to stay close to the source of the water, the

infinite Creator, to nourish our spirit and thus remain in consciousness. Those who fail in this regard, or those who think they are their own god, or think they do not need a direct relationship with the One who created them, will always experience a lack in their lives, an emptiness that they will try to fill with supposedly complete self-realization, but it will never come. The more a person moves away from the Eternal God, the more true happiness and peace move away from them.

Neglecting this point delays blessings. There can be moments when everything seems to be going well, and one does not need anything. Then, the ego regains control of the mind, emotional distress increases, and inner emptiness grows stronger and stronger.

When a person's spirit is neglected and poorly nourished, it is dull, like a drought-stricken and thirsty field in which no life is produced, and it remains asleep, unconscious. Until they give water to their own spirit to drink, they will awaken and begin to live in truth. Even a desert comes to life when water is poured upon it; that barren, lifeless, dusty place becomes fertile and flourishes.

There is a space within each of us that has the form of the Eternal God; nothing and no one else can fill it but him. To understand this is to have the most powerful awakening, for He is the Giver of all good, of every good thing, the One who helps us remain conscious and renew ourselves to attract the greatest blessings ever dreamed of to ourselves and our loved ones.

Feeding your spirit every day accelerates the process of transformation tremendously. Your life becomes a powerful magnet that attracts the good. Peace and a sense of fulfillment remain in your life, not as the fleeting peace and satisfaction that the ego gives, which it snatches away as quickly as it came, filling the soul with anguish and the mind with anxiety, but as the peace that is above any circumstance you may go through. Living in peace and fulfillment is perfectly possible and should be the norm.

The magnetism we radiate is also cumulative. Every thought process in the mind affects that magnetism or energy that comes from within us. When thoughts are directed from the consciousness, they are healthy, and the power of attraction or magnetism of the good is more significant. If thoughts are driven by the ego, they are destructive, and the energy we emit is poisonous, attracting disorder and chaos.

WHEREVER YOU ARE RIGHT NOW, BEGIN TO ATTRACT THE GOOD

It doesn't matter where you are in the process, if you are just beginning your awakening, or if, looking around your life, it seems like you practically have to renovate everything and start from scratch; every tree started from the ground up. Everything in life can get better if you believe in it, but the opposite is also true; the scales tip to where you put your focus.

Every past suffering, every painful and difficult experience, was the process you needed to prepare your fields. Deep down, your spirit was trying to tell you that there was more, that this could not be everything, and that life was slipping through your fingers. Your soul was being held captive by the ego, which had deceived you into believing that it was you. Suffering is not the nature of the human being; it is the result of going against the laws of the Creator. Any of his laws that are broken will bring loss and suffering.

We tend to be beings who forget easily, especially when the ego is in control of the mind because it saturates it with noise, situations to attend to, and unnecessary burdens, until the change, which at some point began, unravels and is lost. We need to be constantly reminded that we are responsible for building and renewing our minds in order to be transformed and remain conscious of choosing the right thoughts.

Knowledge without action is like seeds without planting: it will not bear fruit. The key lies in putting into practice what we learn.

This book is written in a practical and simple language. I have intentionally repeated the same ideas in various ways to emphasize the importance of adopting a healthy mindset so that these ideas become internalized and manifest as your new positive habit. Read the book several times to remind yourself to stay in your process of change and awakening until your mind is completely renewed and your life is transformed into what you are meant to be.

Start tipping the scales in your favor today. Be aware that we go through life sowing with every thought, every word, and every attitude. Focus on what you want, enjoy your life, smile more, and firmly believe that what you want is possible and that it will come without a doubt. In every act you do today, sow what you want to reap tomorrow. Create beautiful moments every day, even something as simple as having a coffee with your family, looking at the stars, or enjoying laughing at something healthy so that your day does not end without having created a beautiful moment to remember.

CHAPTER 9
FIRM MENTAL IMAGES

What a person visualizes in their mind, they are bringing it to life; they are shaping their own life.

It is not a matter of ignoring and neglecting everything we do not like. It is about analyzing what needs to be corrected and resolved, making decisions, and setting limits and goals. This process of analytical thinking directed toward conflict resolution, goal achievement, and evaluation of the way forward is correct and necessary. Once the analysis is done, the appropriate actions are taken, and the mental focus should be on the expected result.

MENTAL IMAGES

Mental images are the ideas produced by your thoughts in a conscious and focused way about what you want in a particular area. They involve visualizing the end result as if you already have it in the present and calling things that are not yet as if they already are.

If you are very shy and you would like to be able to socialize and speak in public without blushing, your throat closing, or feeling very nervous, but you keep thinking about your shyness, so you are programming your subconscious to reinforce this belief, making it even harder to overcome. What you should do is visualize yourself speaking in public in the most natural and relaxed way, enjoying yourself, and imagining that the listeners are listening to you attentively and with pleasure. You can repeat phrases like, "I feel very comfortable speaking in public; it is easy for me to do it, and I enjoy it; it makes me feel very good and I flow."

Let's say you are going through a difficult economic period, and right now, you are having a hard time making payments and making ends meet. If you talk about it at work, with your friends, and when you get home, or if you complain about the prices when you go to buy something, and you have thoughts that money is getting less and less, that everything is getting more and more expensive, and so on, you are sowing that seed of scarcity. You may be right in what you think or say, but the one who is affected by your thoughts and words is yourself.

Talking about scarcity will not get you out of it; on the contrary, you are attracting it more strongly to your daily life. Complaining does not solve or eliminate things; it makes them bigger. The subconscious, which does not question anything that happens in your mind and does not know how to distinguish between what you want and what you do not want, simply takes it as an order that if you are thinking about scarcity, it is because scarcity is what you want—this is called self-sabotage.

Your subconscious will create situations so that your life experience will be the shortage you are thinking of. You will break things, cause something to slip out of your hands and break, have breakdowns in your house or car, leave the water running without noticing, and leave the lights or heat on. This is your subconscious mind obeying your thoughts.

In addition, the energy of your thoughts is thrown out of you, and conditions arise where lack of money, shortages, losses, extra expenses, and unexpected events come at you from all directions every day. I have heard people call this a rough patch or say that it seems like bad things come at them all at once, or that everything is conspiring against them, or that they are having bad luck. It is nothing of the sort; it is simply the result of the mental images they automatically, repetitively, and unconsciously hold in their minds and the seeds they have planted.

The same happens in any relationship: with your partner, with your parents, with your children, or with a friend. If there is something that is not going the way you want it to and you think about it all the time, it creates a mental predisposition to see everything negative, and the subconscious creates some situation for there to be an argument or for the relationship to deteriorate further. In the environment, there will be an uncomfortable atmosphere of tension. The best thing to do is to step back for a moment to give space. We have already seen that nothing works if we try to force it; everything must flow.

If you think and speak badly about a relationship, it will not improve. If your economy is bad, it is because you think and believe negatively about money, perhaps with zeal, greed, or envy. For the outside to change, the inside must change first.

If you have a health problem, follow your doctor's instructions to the letter, but do not make it a topic of conversation with the people around you. First, discard the complaint, as it does not change anything; it only makes the situation worse. Complaining brings curses. Better choose to bless and create firm mental images of good health.

Bless your health, even if it is not optimal at the moment; bless your relationships, money, job, body, food, and the house you live in. When you bless, the power given to you is increased, and your renewal is accelerated.

Begin to visualize the future you want in this instant of the present. The ego has brought enough drama in the past; it is time to rule your own mind, relax, and enjoy life. Make your payments with a feeling of gratitude and love. Imagine owning your own business and being your own boss so you have enough time to do the things in life that are really important to you. Life is not about working to pay bills and struggling to put food on the table; that is the delusion of the ego, and the ego is not you.

At all times, focus on having mental images of what you want, seeing yourself happy, prosperous, free, at peace, and walking in love. What will happen is that you will give your subconscious mind a command of abundance. You will be projecting positive energy outward, connecting with the inexhaustible source of all that is good. Your spirit will then receive ideas, and you will see possibilities that you have previously overlooked.

WE ATTRACT BLESSINGS OR STOP THEM WITH MENTAL IMAGES

The mental pictures in your brain happen every day, every moment, whether you are aware of it or not. Everything you believe brings strength to those mental images you have, and they are activated to become your reality.

Every moment, depending on what is going on in your mind, you are either attracting a blessing or pushing it away. As we are all interconnected through the energy that fills the universe, the blessings that you do not activate within yourself or that you lose also affect others. When you are blessed by consciously orienting your life, blessings flow from you to others, and then you contribute, help, teach, and inspire.

In every situation, always imagine and expect the best possible outcome without hesitation. Wait, seek, and choose the blessing by creating focused images and mental pictures of it. Anything good you can think of for yourself and others can become a reality. It already exists in another dimension, and by following the principles of the Eternal Creator, you can attract it into your reality.

ACTIVATING CORRECT MENTAL PROCESSES

The idea of consciously focusing on what you want is to get to the point where you see it and believe it as your reality, not in the future but in the present. This triggers all the internal processes in both the conscious and subconscious mind, leading you to take concrete actions to make what you are visualizing a reality.

A couple of years ago, I moved into a house I wanted to expand and remodel. One day, I sat down in the living room to think about the changes I planned to make; I visualized where the new large kitchen would be, a library with all my books, the guest bedrooms, the bathrooms, and so forth. I imagined everything in great detail, including the furniture I would put in each place. I didn't do it with the feeling that I would like it to happen by wishing it to happen in the future, but with the full certainty that it already was, I was utterly convinced of it.

Then I got up for a glass of water and naturally made my way to where I had just visualized the new kitchen—my subconscious took what I had just visualized as a present reality. Right now, I am writing this book from this spacious remodeled house, exactly as I imagined it, with every detail and every piece of furniture made a reality.

Today, you reap what you sowed in your mind yesterday, and tomorrow, you will reap what you plant today. Be conscious of planting firm images of what you want in your mind. Visualize happy moments in your relationships and enjoyable times with your loved ones. You must be specific in your mental images so that your brain and mind can work faster on them.

Mental images should not be seen only in the future because they will always remain there; the key is to be convinced without a doubt that they are already a reality. When you firmly believe them, it is only a matter of time before they manifest.

When someone is making a cake, they mix all the ingredients, put it in a mold, and then place it in the oven; they only have to wait for the right amount of time for it to be ready. They don't begin to doubt whether or not there will be a cake in the oven once they open it;

they know, without a doubt, that their delicious cake will be there. While waiting for the cake to be ready, they might prepare coffee or call their family to share it. Thus, with this certainty, you must internalize the conviction of the law of sowing and reaping without doubting and hoping that the mental images you consciously focus on projecting are already a reality.

The worst thing an adult can do is to think that to be mature, one must be serious, dramatic, anxious, and stop having fun. We must always be like children, with the ability to believe without hesitation, to play, to laugh, to have fun, and to get excited about even small details. We must increase our ability to imagine good things and firmly believe that they are possible if we really put our will into them.

At this stage of the process of generating firm mental images, use all your imagination. Play with visualizing everything you want and seeing it in your present reality. Strive to make your life an inspirational movie with a touch of comedy rather than a drama or thriller. Have fun.

Remember that thoughts carry more weight the more they are repeated in the mind until they are internalized. Focus on the transformation process for forty days, practicing daily. You can repeat this cycle as many times as you want, knowing that the more you do it, the easier and faster it will be to get the results you are looking for in each area. Continue with your will fixed on keeping mental images of what you want until you get it.

What gives strength to the mental images of the changes you want to make, both at the level of your thoughts, habits, beliefs, and emotions, of what you want to do and what you want to achieve, is that you do not see it in your mind as a wish, a fantasy, or something you would like to happen, but visualize it with the complete certainty that you already have it.

Activate your faith and reduce the infinite possibilities to make the decision to believe and trust. Faith firmly believes and attracts the future into the present. It is to give form to what has no form; it is to make possible what the ego makes you think is impossible. And according to what you believe, according to your faith, it will always be done, no more and no less.

CHAPTER 10

THINKING > FEELING > TAKING ACTION > MANIFESTATION

Any transformation within ourselves and any external change in any area of our lives begins in the mind, thinking, feeling strongly, and taking concrete action about it.

By renewing the mind, thoughts are inclined toward the healthy and positive, and the energy and power they emit are multiplied because we are helped by our spirit, which is united to the greatest inexhaustible source of power in the universe: The Creator.

THINKING

The first step is thinking. It is being aware and choosing focused thoughts of what we want.

The renewal of the mind takes place with a conscious and deliberate way of thinking, focused on the solution and on the end result, creating firm mental images of what we want to achieve.

We must be specific and constant when forming mental images. We must take time each day to focus and visualize those changes we want. You can even do this while you are waiting for your turn at the bank or anywhere else. See yourself as already being, doing, and having what you are firmly convinced you want.

FEELING

After thinking about what you want and generating mental pictures, the second step is to feel it firmly as your reality.

Feelings are hundreds of times more potent than thoughts; they emit a powerful energy that transcends space and brings consequences (harvest) beyond the present time. These are things that must be understood with the mind of the spirit.

All emotions already exist within you and are activated by a thought. When you imagine what you want, feelings of well-being are triggered, and this is what you are looking for in this part of the process: to feel your best most of the time.

Taking the time to meditate on the change you are working toward in every facet of your life activates the feeling of having what you want in the present moment. Remember that the subconscious interprets everything you think and imagine as a present reality. Use this tool to your advantage to create feelings of happiness and pleasure and to motivate yourself with the feeling that you have already achieved it.

You should seek to feel your best, staying focused and aware. This does not mean turning a blind eye to the situations you need to attend to, but that once you have done your part, you choose to return to an inner state of well-being, thinking about what pleases you and what you want in life. Use reminders to help you stay in consciousness and take moments to stop and enjoy.

On a table in my library at home, there is a box of tea that I brought back from London on one of my previous trips. When I see it, it always reminds me to take a moment to rest and relax, to have tea or coffee with my family. I also have written reminders and placed photos that help me to stay aware of choosing peace no matter what is happening outside and to make pauses during the day to enjoy and expand the feeling of well-being and of already having in the present the goals I want at that moment.

Make writings and stick them on the mirror, put reminders on your cell phone; always be aware that you control your mind, not the other way around. Take small breaks during the day to relax and to increase a feeling of well-being inside you. Don't wait for reasons to feel happy; find reasons to be happy every day. Create good moments, sit down to enjoy a cup of tea in the garden, play with your pet, or call or visit a loved one. Make it a habit to create a beautiful moment before the day ends. Feeling good is one of the best signs that you are conscious and in the creative process.

Surround yourself with beautiful things; if you like flowers, buy them and put them in front of you. Use your best silverware and wear your best clothes without waiting for a special occasion. What better reason to celebrate than the fact that you are alive, that you are beginning to be more conscious, and that you are in the process of renewing your mind and transforming your life?

TAKING ACTION

After consciously thinking about the changes you want and feeling them as if they are already happening right now comes the third step, which is to take action.

No significant achievement will come if any of the steps are skipped or not done correctly. If you have a dream or a goal, and you think about it, wish for it, and visualize it, but you sit back and do nothing, nothing will happen. Action is required. Faith without action is not alive. You cannot believe something without acting, without doing something about what you believe in.

I have met countless people who have stopped at the first two steps. They wanted to make some change in their lives, change a habit, quit an addiction, or achieve some material goal or accomplishment. They thought about it and visualized it daily; they felt the desire to achieve what they dreamed of, but there was cognitive dissonance. Their actions were contrary to their thoughts and feelings.

This usually happens when people ignore what we have learned in the previous chapters. They have not let go of attachments or replaced limiting beliefs; they have not had inner healing, they live in victimization, and they believe that the voice of the ego in their minds is their own. They have not had a powerful awakening. So, they develop behaviors that are inconsistent with what they really want.

They live in competition to get what they want, and competition means sending the message that there is not enough to go around, as if everyone wants the same thing and has to fight and battle to get it. This distorts the energy in their environment, and they project envy, falsehood, and appearance, causing the ego to take over.

When you live that way, things reach a limit at some point, there is a ceiling, or something starts to go wrong in some areas of your life. Maybe they acted with envy or made a deal that affected someone else, thinking only of their own benefit, and sometime later, their marital relationship deteriorates. Even if you don't see the connection between one thing and the other, sowing a bad seed brings a bad harvest. Everything, without exception, that you do or wish for others, you end up attracting into your own life.

Everything must be done with honesty and love. You cannot wish for something that is detrimental to another. If, at this moment, you are doing some business or deal that only benefits you and affects others negatively, you must change that immediately; even if you seem to be doing well now, the harvest will come later; the law of compensation never fails. For the blessing to follow us every day of our lives, our scales must be fair in all our dealings.

It is not only thinking and feeling as if you already have what you want, but you should start acting as if what you want already is, not as if one day it might come to be. There must be congruence between your thoughts and feelings and your actions. Make decisions, make changes, and act toward what you firmly desire as if you already have it in this present moment. At first, it will seem strange to act in a different way or without seeing at that moment what you want to achieve or the change within you because it is something new, but if you remain firm in your consciousness and there is congruence between what happens in your mind and your actions, there is no doubt that what you want will be.

Take actions that help your mind believe that what you want is already a reality in your present. If you want a house, go see houses you like, take pictures of them, visualize the furniture you will put in each room, buy the picture you will hang over the fireplace. If you want to go on a trip, buy things you will need on your trip. If you want new clothes, make room in your closet. If you want a partner, make room in the closet for their things, and so on.

FAITH REQUIRES ACTION

Everything is possible for the one who believes. Your life is a set of beliefs, and you act on them. You go to your job or business every morning because you believe that at the end of the week, you will receive your reward, your pay. No one would work for a month if they didn't believe they would be paid for their work. Believing without doing something is to go backward. In every situation and circumstance, you will always have the option of believing or doubting.

Faith is an engine that drives us to action and is ignited by the spirit. By filling the mind with the things of the spirit, faith grows. On the contrary, the ego is hesitant and unbelieving; therefore, its action is not directed toward obtaining clear and positive objectives but toward appearance. It works to stagnate the person in the emotional whirlpool and chaos—complete opposites. You act according to what you really believe inside.

Faith without action is illusory, it does not exist, it is fantasy, it is self-deception. There are two options: believe the voice of the ego in the mind or believe the inner voice of the spirit. When a challenge presents itself, choose to listen to your true voice and believe without hesitation that just as things in the past have been resolved, whatever you are going through today will also be resolved. The more you work on being conscious, the better and faster the situations you face will be settled.

All actions should be done without haste. You don't want to overload yourself with activities because you feel an urgency to achieve your inner transformation or your outer goals. This causes anxiety, and anxiety delays lasting results. Each day brings its own challenges; you must remain in the present moment and find time to rest, meditate, and enjoy nature, family, the sky, and the stars. If in your daily life, you cannot find at least thirty minutes as a gift to yourself and have a moment of relaxation, you are in busyness, and there is something wrong with your priorities. You need to make the necessary corrections. We need time for distraction.

One should not live in anxiety and be overloaded with occupations, but neither should one procrastinate and leave things accumulated for the next day. Of course, here comes the criterion of each person, and each one must evaluate what must be done today and what can wait.

If you're doing something you don't enjoy and you feel exhausted and sad, it's time to evaluate whether you should continue with it or look for new alternatives. Also, analyze where your mind is when you do each activity. Doing something with complaint or anger or thinking about negative things both in the past and in the future makes the moment bland and tiring, and time passes slowly.

Don't waste your present moments in a state of self-hypnosis focused on the things of the past or the future. Your true and only real life is in the present.

ACTUAL MANIFESTATION OF MENTAL IMAGES

After focused and conscious thinking, feeling, and believing it as if it were already in the present and taking concrete actions, comes the fourth step, which is to wait for it to manifest without any doubt.

During the creative process of renewing the mind to transform our inner and outer lives, we have learned the actions to take step by step. First, we cleared the ground by removing all attachments and beliefs that are not functional. We have pulled out the weeds of the ego in the mind and laid a firm foundation by getting rid of victimization and placing strong stones at the base, taking responsibility for our own decisions and actions and for our well-being and happiness.

At this stage of the process, we must be careful to stay in consciousness and direct our thoughts, feelings, and actions toward the objective we are trying to achieve, waiting without hesitation.

A person who is divided within themselves will struggle to remain focused on a specific goal. They will be inconsistent in their actions, like a leaf carried by the wind from one side to the other. One day, they may feel enthusiastic about their transformation and believe that their desires have become a reality. However, they may doubt their changes, themselves, and what they truly want the next day.

We all have good and not-so-good moments. We have already learned that emotions cannot be hidden or ignored because what we keep quiet today, the body will shout it later. We must take a few minutes to live this emotion, learn to let go, forgive, not listen to the voice of the ego, and consciously focus the mind on the present moment, on what is healthy and positive.

You can go back to the first chapters of the book as many times as you need to until you let go of all attachments and forgive yourself and everyone else. It is not a race; you are not in competition with anyone; it is about your most precious asset: your own life. Until you are completely healed, do not give up. You were given the power to renew your life, and the greatest achievement we can reach is to conquer ourselves, to have a happy and blissful inner life, to live in peace and prosper in everything.

It is not a matter of concentrating on achieving external changes, because that is what the ego has been doing all our lives, nor is it a matter of accumulating material things and personal achievements because that would not bring any inner well-being; we would feel a greater emptiness again in a short time. What we are looking for in the first place is a renewal inside, in the mind, in the emotions so that we can be free of all the stormy past and all internal whirlwinds. Only then will true prosperity manifest itself internally and externally.

From now on, the material things that come into your life will no longer be to try to fill voids, please your ego, or pretend before other people. They will be to make life more comfortable for you and those you love, to selflessly help others so that the greatest number of people know that they can have a powerful awakening and transform their lives for the better.

Sometimes, manifestation happens instantly. For example, changing your mood is very easy by focusing on something you love, something beautiful, or making a mental list of all the things you are grateful for.

Other times, it takes a period of time for things or changes to manifest, but even that waiting time is a good thing because it strengthens your faith, or maybe you change your mind and want something different or to modify what you want to achieve.

Always remember that happiness is something that

comes from within and depends solely on you. It's not the responsibility of anyone else to make you happy. Expecting others to do so would be selfish, as it puts an unfair burden on them that they cannot fulfill. It would be momentary, external happiness that would return you to attachments.

The worst mistake you can make is to give up. The most infallible way to achieve success is to always try one more time until the result comes. Think it one more time, feel it one more time, visualize it one more time, and take action one more time until your renewal, your transformation, your dream manifests. Anything is possible if you can believe it.

THE POWER OF WORDS

The Eternal has also given power to our words; with them, we can bless or curse; with each word, we sow good or bad seed. Remember that even a fool is counted as wise when they are silent, and those who speak much add evil to their own lives. We should always think before we speak if what we are going to say will edify and be a blessing for us and those who are listening or if it is the ego speaking, wanting to victimize, justify, or aggrandize itself. There is power in your words, and everything that is said is a seed that will give you a harvest.

A good word spoken at the right time is like a balm that can heal profound wounds. Words loaded with anger, victimization, and judgment are like swords that deeply damage both the one who says them and the one who receives them. Although we have already seen how to work with labels and external attacks, a bad word said by us or received from someone we love will always have a negative impact.

We can use our words to give blessings. It is not about speaking lightly from the ego because that would be egocentric, materialistic statements that would only add negativity instead of blessing. I know many people who live in the ego, and every day, they make positive statements for their lives, and although they have repeated them for years and years, they have not had any significant changes. Their lives are an emotional storm; they live in scarcity, from problem to problem or stuck.

As long as the ego rules and attachments and limiting beliefs are not broken, there will be cognitive dissonance. You can spend a lifetime making statements, but you will only be wasting your breath. There is an order to everything, and there are basic principles that we must consider to lead a harmonious and prosperous life in everything.

This book contains the information of many years of study, research, courses, and certifications, of reading hundreds of books, of preparation, of experience working with patients, with myself, of many hours spent in fasting and prayer, and the results are summarized as much as possible to make it simple and easy to read and apply so that each reader has the basic tools to renew their mind and transform their life. All of these steps are necessary for integral wellness in the mind, in the emotions, in making peace with the past, with oneself, with relationships, and with the environment. To project the power the Eternal gave us and attract blessings of all kinds to our lives. Skipping or ignoring part of the process will only bring incongruence; the person will remain like the caterpillar that could not get out of its chrysalis.

A house without a roof doesn't work, nor does one without doors and windows or a foundation. It may not be much fun at first, but it's all a necessary process. Your life is like a house under construction; no step can be skipped or ignored to make the final result extraordinary.

The affirmations we make with our words must be made consciously, coming from the spirit, with complete certainty that what we are declaring is already a reality.

INACTION WEAKENS THE PROCESS

Ideas and beliefs become stronger the more we think about them. Thoughts accumulate significance until they are ingrained in our minds. When a strong feeling is added to these mental images, it motivates action because we firmly believe in what we think. When we practice this daily, change begins to happen. We wait for things to manifest, not with our arms folded, but by putting action to our faith.

In reality, by thinking, feeling, and acting, we are being transformed; internal changes are occurring, and we are projecting a powerful signal outward. It is like a photographic camera: What you focus on will be what is captured in the photograph. Thoughts are mental images that join the creative energy that fills the universe and return to us the exact manifestation of the photographs we project into the mind.

When the images we project are not constant, that is, when they are not practiced daily for at least forty days, the thought processes at the cerebral level weaken because they are like trees that first sprout and begin to grow, forming cerebral ramifications that need to be watered in order to complete their process and affirm themselves. This is achieved by thinking about what we want on a daily basis, feeling it, and adding action.

Action strengthens inner change and accelerates outer manifestation. On the contrary, inaction weakens the inner processes until they disappear and prevents what we want to manifest on a physical level.

We see many people who start projects and don't finish them. They either leave them incomplete or lose interest after a brief period of time, or they get excited about something, but the ego takes over, and they convince themselves that they don't have enough time to continue. They are constantly moving from one idea to another, from one decision to another. They don't give the brain time to work properly to form new neural branches that lead to real change.

Everything is a whole, a balance. Transforming a life requires physical, neural, cellular, and thought changes, replacing beliefs and letting go of attachments, victimization, and unforgiveness. It also requires external work and action. It all starts in the mind, but it must be followed by action. What is believed in the mind is put into practice.

What are the next steps you need to take to put your transformation into action? Even if someone gives you a gift, it is necessary to stretch out your hands to receive it. Every physical manifestation of what you want requires an action of faith that you must begin to take today. It is you who can renew or stop and sabotage your own transformation. Your dream, your inner transformation, the renewal of your mind, and what you want to achieve in life are already there; they are yours; reach out and take them. Believe without doubting.

CHAPTER 11
SMASHING THE BRONZE SKIES

LOVE AND GRATITUDE

A lot of people seem to have a figurative lock or bronze sky over them, something that stops the rain and prevents their fields from being watered so that good seeds can grow and produce a bountiful harvest. Despite following some of the steps I share in this book, their skies remain closed. Let's look at several things that could cause such barriers, preventing the rain, the blessing from entering our lives.

Everything must be done consciously, not mechanically, as the ego does. Everything we have seen so far is necessary. We cannot neglect to feed the spirit because then the ego will not be extinguished; neither can we skip to work on releasing attachments and replacing limiting beliefs or neglect to be aware of the seeds we sow with thoughts, emotions, words, and actions, for then the heavens will close so that the abundant rain will not fall. We may receive some raindrops, some changes, and improvements, but we are not looking for something half-hearted; we are looking for a total transformation. We want the full blessing and a full and abundant life in all good things.

Many people delude themselves into thinking that they have already forgiven someone, but they take every opportunity to treat them with sarcasm, criticize them, make claims, or speak ill of them, and this is because they have not really let go; they have not truly forgiven. They continue to victimize themselves and believe that this gives them the power to criticize and condemn.

I have heard people say countless times the phrases "I am very sincere, and I say what I think," "I judge with fair judgment," or "I am telling the truth." However, they immediately proceed to make negative or critical comments about someone else, and this is done with an attitude of unforgiveness, victimization, or self-justification. Pointing out the mistakes of others does not correct them, and the law of compensation will not analyze whether we are right or wrong in the negative things we say; it will simply give us back something similar. Negativity attracts negativity.

When we understand that we have not been put here to be anyone's judge, we begin to awaken, and it becomes easier to let go of the burdens and move forward in our own transformation.

There is a lot of power in the words that we speak. If we do not stop our words from saying negative things, it activates other mechanisms in the ego that implant suggestions in the mind of something negative that produces pleasure. For example, if someone struggles with addiction to cigarettes, alcohol, pornography, video games, food, or compulsive shopping, and they don't filter their words, speaking poorly about others (whether or not they have a reason to do so), it does not stop there as this can trigger the ego to crave a drink, cigarette, unhealthy food, etcetera.

You can tell from the way the person is speaking whether it is the ego that has taken control of the mind or whether it is the person's true essence that is speaking.

Your true self does not judge, does not criticize. It can see the negative in others, but instead of pointing a finger, it feels compassion when it sees others tormented and numbed by their own ego in the mind. And they feel the desire to help them wake up so that they can become conscious and begin to truly live.

Those who are able to control their mouth and their words are also able to control their whole body. Their mind is no longer under the influence of the ego, and they have conquered themselves and are fully conscious of their true self.

Now, we understand that our responsibility is to work with ourselves; the focus is on our inner work. Remember that there is no true love in the ego, and love is required to forgive and heal. Any change will be superficial and temporary when the person has not turned off the ego. Healing will not be complete and profound. At some point, the ego will find a trigger to bring out all the pent-up anger, sadness, or any emotion that has not been truly healed.

An unfaithful husband may not see the connection between his wrongdoing and the economic shortage he is experiencing, or some illness. Someone who constantly complains, speaks ill of others, makes claims of anything, does a favor to collect it in the future, or complains for the help they gave may not see the connection between the bad seed they are sowing and the feeling of loneliness they face, the bad interpersonal relationships they have, or the constant physical discomforts.

Everything is sowing and reaping. Even the smallest and most trivial act has positive or negative consequences, first within, then in the environment and beyond. Whatever is done or said against someone, even if the person thinks they are correct and in their right, everything negative that is said about others will close the heavens above and turn them to bronze. The rain will not fall, and the good seed will not be able to germinate and grow. Blessings will be blocked.

LOVE

Nothing can break the bronze skies more easily than love. Nothing has greater inner healing power than love. Nothing can transform a life more efficiently than love. Faith can make things that seem impossible happen. Hope can become the motivation that helps us get up after a fall and drives us to keep going when our strength seems to be running out. But there is nothing greater than love. Love is the most powerful force that exists in the entire universe.

When we love, we emit the highest positive energy signal that transcends space. It is the most powerful attracting force.

Love is a fruit of the spirit. It develops when we feed our spirit by connecting directly with the Creator. When we neglect our spiritual nourishment, the ego immediately takes control of the mind to sow its bad seed, distract us from the good, focus our thoughts on the bad and the external, and torment us emotionally and mentally. The most effective antidote to the ego is love.

We must love every minute of our lives, everything we do, and every person we have with us. Walking in love makes us flow, things stop seeming monotonous, and life stops being heavy and becomes enjoyable. Then renewal and transformation are affirmed.

Love transforms what would otherwise be unlikely, difficult, slow, or impossible. I have seen situations, people, relationships, and whole lives completely transformed by love. Moody, disobedient teenagers who were changed not by a lecture, a punishment, or an imposition but by the power of love.

Love not only adds up; it multiplies. A gesture of pure love, a hug, a smile, or a good word said at the right moment can heal a hardened, hurt, insecure, or needy heart. Words like "I love you," "I am sorry," "Thank you," and "Please," spoken from the depths of a sincere heart and charged with love, are a healing torrent for the one who says them and for the one who receives them.

It is extremely important to know that sometimes, to love, you also have to take a step back, stop forcing something, and give freedom and space. Love flows; it is not something imposed or demanded.

All the blessings, all that is true, all that is good, all that is pure, and all that renews is directly linked to love. Where there is love, things flourish and prosper. What you put love into grows, multiplies, and you draw it to you. Even a meal made with love tastes different. A polite smile is not the same as a smile full of love. Feel love for life, for nature, for what you do, for those around you, for the Creator of all. Remember that love can only enter and grow in your life through your spirit, which in turn receives it from the inexhaustible source of love, the Creator of the universe; He is love, and from him emanates every good and every blessing.

In this step of giving love, do not forget to give it to yourself. Treat yourself well, with respect and dignity, and with nice and kind words. Self-love includes taking care of your thoughts and emotions, your eating habits, your sleep schedule, your exercise, your interpersonal relationships, and giving yourself time to rest.

Enjoy your company. Don't have music or noise all the time when you are alone. The ego can't stand you listening to your true inner voice lest it be discovered. When the ego dominates the thoughts, there will always be mental noise; it will not want you to be silent and will immediately suggest that you turn on music or television or call someone on the phone. Learn to enjoy silence and your own company. If a person cannot stand themselves, others will not enjoy their company either.

It is the ego that can't stand itself and that prevents you from enjoying and loving yourself. Instead, it resorts to various tactics to seek approval from others, such as giving gifts and throwing parties; it tries to give or do something to keep people on its side and even uses victimization to get the attention of others. From there, blackmail and manipulation arise, and the person becomes dramatic and bitter. All this is a lack of self-love.

Doing things without love is like sowing seeds and not watering them. Every step of the way, we go through life giving or withholding love. The emotional state in which you find yourself at this moment is the result of the love you have unconsciously given or denied. Love yourself, others, and everything you do. When you give love, you add and multiply in your life and in the lives of others; when you refuse to give love, you subtract from yourself and from others.

The more the spirit is nourished, the more love will flow from you, and then, the ego becomes more and more extinguished. The past ceases to be your present. You no longer seek approval from others, forgiveness becomes natural, and there is no longer time or place for drama, complaints, gossip, or resentment. The anxiety of the future disappears because love brings confidence and rest. Your soul ceases to be constantly tormented by the ego; love brings freedom and life.

When you love, life flows to your organs, brain, skin, every molecule, and corner of your being. You become an alarm clock that inspires others to have a powerful awakening.

If you focus on giving just one thing in life, give love. It will change everything for you, for those around you, and even far beyond.

FEAR DESTROYS LOVE

The opposite of love is fear, and fear comes directly from the ego. Fear is not our nature. We can feel fear in the face of danger, which is fine because it helps our organism enter a state of alertness to preserve life and flee from danger. On the other hand, to live with fear is to live without love; it is to be a prisoner of the ego in our own mind.

Fear causes a person to live in a state of unconsciousness; reality is distorted, and they live in darkness, where things seem bigger and scarier. They take their eyes off what they want and put them on what they do not want, which is the bad and negative. Fear paralyzes, sinks, and enslaves. But love casts out fear.

Love is something that grows and transforms. When we make the conscious decision to love, we position ourselves at the highest level above the ego. Nothing is above love because the Creator of all is love itself.

Eagles are characterized by flying at great heights. When they carry their younglings, they place them on top because they know that above them, there are no predators; the other birds fly below them. The ego makes us fly low, in a constant state of fear, as if lulled into unconsciousness; it clips our wings. On the contrary, love is like wings that lift us above all fear. The one who loves has no fear, because they position themselves above all that is temporal, fleeting, and illusory. An eagle that soars to the heights flies calmly without worrying about the storms that may be below it.

GRATITUDE

When combined with love, gratitude has spectacular power. It can instantly focus the mind on what is healthy and positive. If you're having a bad day, take a few minutes to consciously focus on what you're grateful for, and you'll see an immediate change in your mood.

Gratitude also multiplies the blessing. Everything you are grateful for grows and strengthens, whether it is a relationship, your health, money, or everything else. If someone gives you a cup of coffee or a hug every morning, but you never say thank you, the person will stop doing it at some point. If, on the other hand, you say thank you sincerely and with a smile, you encourage that act to strengthen and also motivate you to do something for that person.

Love and gratitude are not passive; they drive you to action. When you love, you act. When you are grateful for something, it starts an engine that drives you to take care of and water what you are grateful for.

Every morning when you wake up, develop the habit of giving thanks. Instead of picking up your cell phone and looking at social networks or answering messages, first, be thankful and prepare your soil so that the seed does not fall among stones and thorns. Gratitude is not directed to the universe because the universe is a creation; we thank the Creator of the universe and everything that exists.

Our true nature is to remain in a state of awareness, love, and gratitude. We are not designed to endure negative emotions for long; the body goes into a state of turmoil. When we experience stress or anxiety, the body releases cortisol, which is the main stress hormone. It takes several hours for cortisol to be eliminated from the body, causing the immune system to weaken, leading to stomach problems, indigestion, respiratory problems, and allergies; it also inflames the most sensitive parts of the body and causes pain in the teeth, neck, back, and stomach.

Before, when we remained asleep in the unconsciousness of the ego, we were inclined to a negative expectation of fatalism, with the fear and anxiety of thinking that something terrible could happen to us or those we love. When you live loving and grateful, the opposite happens; it fosters an expectation of good; you no longer expect bad things to happen in your life, and now you hope and believe that something good will happen to you every day. This is staying in consciousness from the spirit.

The more gratitude you feel and the more love you give, the better you will feel; you will become like a magnet that attracts all that is good. This is not just a way of saying things; you literally begin to attract good things because you are sowing a seed of the highest quality and radiating positive energy.

Being grateful helps us stay in the present, and the more conscious we are, the more the ego, which is the worst enemy of a transformed and happy life, is extinguished. The ego cannot and will never be happy because it is based on fear, and as we have already mentioned, fear destroys love.

THE EGO TRIES TO PUT LOCKS ON YOUR TRANSFORMATION

The person living in the ego puts resistance to feeding their spirit; the ego convinces the person that it is a waste of time, feels uncomfortable, gets distracted, feels anger and rejection toward their own spirit, and self-deceives themselves by looking outside for what they can only find within.

If you lose your car keys inside your house, it would be absurd to look for them at the neighbor's house across the street; they are not there, and you will not find them even if you spend your whole life looking for them. Nothing external can replace the internal. Material or external things come practically by themselves when we wake up. They are extras that, when you receive them, lose their importance compared to the remarkable transformation of a free, renewed, and happy life.

The ego thinks and wants everything to revolve around it; it does not want to change. It seeks that the circumstances and the people around it change so that it can feel momentarily good. That is why it makes people go through life finding faults, identifying what others are doing wrong, what they should correct and change, taking away, subtracting, influencing, and locking up the blessings. Going in this direction is the opposite of love; it is to walk a sterile and deserted path.

Understanding that your true essence, your soul, and your spirit are eternal helps you see things from another perspective. We are here in passing, a brief moment, learning, experiencing, growing, maturing, awakening. Nothing here in this world is as important or as dramatic as the ego leads us to believe. What happens inside you, in your consciousness, is of eternal relevance. The body will, eventually, cease to exist; it is your essence that remains forever.

Unfortunately, many people will realize until the body ceases to exist that they were not the ego, that the ego was the great deceiver that incited them to think, believe, and do things that only frustrated their lives and kept them from being truly free and happy. Let us cultivate a sense of urgency to help others awaken and be free of their ego. What greater act of love is there than helping someone become free from the heavy chains and burdens of attachments and guilt?

Let us take advantage of every instant of the present to be happy, to love, and to be grateful; then, every lock will be opened, and every bronze sky will be broken to let fall all kinds of blessings.

CHAPTER 12
ACCELERATING BLESSINGS

Nothing can speed up blessings and propel our transformation faster than helping others. Helping others with their needs is also a way to feed our spirit. In addition, when we help, we shut down the ego, focus on the needs of others, increase self-esteem, reduce mental noise, feel useful, balance our mood, develop new social skills, and strengthen our immune system.

I encourage you to get involved in some volunteer work or help in your community, such as going to a nursing home or an orphanage, cleaning up a park, picking up trash from the beach, or protecting an endangered species or forest. You do not need to seek to belong to a group or association; you can do it on your own. Go out on the street and look for someone in need and buy them food, give them supplies or clothes, or visit someone who lives alone and share a moment with them. The important thing is to make it a habit rather than something that happens sporadically.

We have already learned that thoughts, feelings, words, and actions are not neutral; with them, we build or tear down, contribute or take away, and move forward or backward. In every encounter with any person, we have the opportunity to be conscious and to add and contribute something to their life—a word, a smile, something that helps them start their awakening process. When you help someone, you add to their life and multiply in your own.

HELPING OTHERS TO WAKE UP

Cultivating and fertilizing the soil are fundamental steps to helping a seed grow. Likewise, when we have awakened to consciousness, we quickly feel the need, urgency, and even responsibility to share what we have learned with others so that they can transform their own lives.

Of course, both parties must be awake to have an effective conversation. Talking to a sleeping person would be just a monologue.

Have you ever had a conversation with someone with whom you tried to share an idea that you knew would be beneficial to that person, and after an enthusiastic explanation on your part, the other person reacted as if you had said nothing? Well, this is because most people are hypnotized by the ego and find it extremely difficult to openly receive something that will benefit their lives so that they can be renewed and transformed.

Now that we are on our awakening and transformation path, we understand that to have a healthy and productive conversation with someone and share ideas, projects, beliefs, business, and so on, the other person must also have a powerful awakening. Otherwise, the ego will intervene and do its sabotage work to rob them of any significant progress they may have in any area. It is difficult to talk freely with someone who is emotionally and spiritually oppressed, and it usually ends in an argument or a search for a way to get away as quickly as possible and with a sense of burden.

The totality of people who live in emotional whirlpools, in anguish, in mental and spiritual torment, with their souls held captive, in economic misery, unhappy, frustrated, and mired in monotony, are people who are ignorant of many or perhaps all of the things we have talked about in this book. They do not have a basic understanding of how they, their mind, their emotions, their soul, their spirit function, and the role the ego plays in deceiving and misleading a person into believing it is their voice. They do not know that they have the power of choice in the mind and that by renewing their mind, their life is transformed. You and I were in the same situation before until we had an awakening thanks to the Eternal Creator.

People need to know that there is a way out of the difficult situations they face, that they can improve their relationship with themselves and those around them, that they can be free from the past, that they can let go of all attachments and choose to believe and hope for the good, discarding all limiting beliefs from the past. There is enough happiness, love, money, peace, and beautiful things to enjoy life.

People miss out on all these blessings by ignoring the truth, focusing on filling the internal with the external, and not knowing their structure. Ignorance steals and holds back blessings.

UNEXPECTED ACTS OF KINDNESS

I have seen people who, when they go to give some kind of help, want trumpets and fanfare. The help we give should be selfless. Although we know that what we add to others multiplies in our own lives, that should not be the reason we help because it creates cognitive dissonance and creates obstacles that nullify the blessing. Giving help with the expectation of receiving a reward turns the skies to bronze because feelings and intentions send out a negative signal, even if what is done is good.

Try to do unexpected acts of kindness for people you know and people you don't know. Pay for coffee for the person behind you in line or the toll for the car behind you. Ask for an extra meal when you go to a restaurant and look for someone on the street who needs it. Give a copy of this book to people you love and also to strangers. Pay the cell phone or electric bill of someone you love. Do not do it thinking about whether they deserve it or not, because that would be the ego coming back. Do it all out of love without expecting a reward from the people you help. Your reward comes only by applying the laws that the Eternal has established in the universe, and as you help others, you accelerate your blessings, and they multiply.

You will see how your life is transformed. Blessing will come to you from all sides until you feel like weeping with joy for the fantastic life you now have.

TIME IS PERFECT

We would have liked to have known all of this years ago, but there is a time for everything. What happened to you in the past was necessary to prepare you for this present moment when you are ready to have a transformation and to be able to properly handle the abundant blessing that is on its way to every area of your life. Perhaps if this knowledge had come earlier, you would not have been ready to receive it and begin your transformation process.

Now, you consciously understand that no one can do the work of renewing your mind for you, nor can you do it for others. However, as we awaken, we see more clearly the need for those around us to awaken as well.

No one who is asleep can be conscious, and no one who has awakened and is conscious can resist the urge to reach out and touch those they love who are asleep. For those who know what is right and do not act, they are hindering their own blessings.

I encourage you to join the mission to help awaken as many people as possible. May they be free of ego and unnecessary burdens, may they begin to live a life free of drama and inner conflicts, and may they be happy. At the end of the day, as we are all interconnected, the freedom of those around us is also part of our own. By recommending this book in your social media, you will help and enrich others while multiplying and accelerating your own blessings.

AUTOMATION IN YOUR NEW LIFE

When you learned to ride a bike, it wasn't the first time you tried it that you could do it; it was through practice, through experience. Your brain created mental images, learned from mistakes and falls until you learned to maintain balance and coordination of your body. Then, you developed the ability to do it naturally, without the need to think about it. The process became automatic.

In the same way, what may seem a little difficult today in your process of renewing your mind and transforming your life will begin to seem natural and fluid as you begin to do it little by little. For this reason, I reiterate the need to read this book as many times as necessary so that the new form of positive thinking takes on the necessary weight to be internalized and thus help your mind in the war to dethrone the ego and remain in consciousness.

No achievement is more important than conquering your own mind; that is where everything begins and where everything that has hurt you throughout your life can end. From there, you can start to create new neuronal ramifications, new ideas, and healthy beliefs about yourself and the world around you. In your mind, you can send out very powerful signals through your thoughts that will return to you in the form of experiences what you consciously and purposefully think from the spirit.

Focus on staying aware of your thoughts during the forty-day process. In that time, work on letting go of all attachments and unnecessary burdens, on replacing all limiting beliefs with healthy and functional beliefs, on improving your personal habits, and on being aware that you are sowing seeds in every instant and that we go through life adding or subtracting, giving love or denying it, building up or tearing down. Affirm the mental images of the new life you want, feel it and believe it without doubting that it is already so, and act according to the new nature of your beliefs. Be grateful for everything at all times.

Commit yourself and repeat the forty-day cycles you deem necessary until you have a complete renewal. Do not give up at any time. You may stumble and fall, but do not allow yourself to remain on the ground; get up and keep going until you reach a point where your life can only be described as spectacular!

In a beautiful forest with majestic and enormous trees, there lived one who was different from all the others. Outwardly, he was the same as the others, and no one would have been able to tell the difference by looking at them. The difference was on the inside.

This unique tree had a dream of becoming something significant, of contributing in some way to the world, and of helping people in need. He spent his days thinking that perhaps he could help people in far-off, frigid regions stay warm during the winter by providing his wood.

He also imagined becoming a cabin that would shelter

a homeless family. In this way, he would be delighted to shelter them and see them happy with their own wooden house.

While dreaming of these and many other things, he always maintained an enthusiastic attitude, wanting to contribute and add, and was determined to give love first and foremost. So when he saw birds flying through the forest, he would invite them to rest for a while and perch on his branches. He would tell them about his dreams and ask them to spread his seeds in other places so that more trees would be born.

He knew that we are all connected somehow and that we need each other for everything to work well. He explained to the birds, who listened intently, that when a tree is cut down, others must be planted in its place because the oxygen they release helps humans breathe, and the carbon dioxide humans exhale is converted by the trees into more oxygen.

He also invited the forest animals to relax under his shade during the hot summer days and to take shelter under his branches on rainy and stormy days.

One day, he saw some lumberjacks in uniforms, who looked like they belonged to a big company, walking through the forest, looking carefully at all the trees until they finally picked him out and took him away. As they went on their way, the tree was not nervous; on the contrary, he was very excited and happy because he knew that somehow what he had dreamed of was coming true. Was he going to help families in remote and frozen places to keep warm during the winter? Or would they turn him into a hut to shelter a family?

When they arrived at their destination, he saw a huge factory. Inside it, they made him go through several processes; it was not easy at all. First, they cut off all his branches, then they took out his fibers, which were later turned into a pulp, and finally, he was turned into sheets of paper. But not just any paper, no! He became the sheets of paper of the book you are holding in your hands right now. The tree was extremely happy!

Dear reader, both the tree with a dream of helping others and the author of this book, written with much love, invite you to join us in the vision of helping many lives in places near and far, cold and warm, to have a powerful awakening of consciousness so that they can renew their minds and transform their lives, just as your life is being transformed as well. My daily prayer is for this to be so. Thank you!

ACKNOWLEDGMENTS

First of all, my greatest, deepest, and most constant thanks to the Creator and Eternal God; I thank him for giving me life, for using me as an inkwell in his hand to write this book, and for absolutely everything I owe to him.

I am thankful for my most precious treasure, which is my family. I give thanks for having the best job in the world, helping lives. Thank you to every person who reads this book. My prayer every morning is that your mind is renewed and your life transformed for the better in all areas, that the ego will always remain subdued, and that you will always remain conscious, directing your mind toward the healthy, the good, and the pure; that your true essence will always live in fullness and flourish in all things.

I thank each of you who share this book with others so that thousands of people can be freed and live in happiness, peace, prosperity, and fulfillment.

Thanks to everyone who contributed, directly or indirectly, to bringing this book to light. Thank you all for everything!

poderosodespertar@gmail.com

(English and Spanish)

www.ingramcontent.com/pod-product-compliance
Lightning Source LLC
Chambersburg PA
CBHW032118040426
42449CB00005B/191